16⁹⁵

84-1372

84-1372

HF5721   Booker, Dianna Daniels
.B63   Send me a memo.

SEND ME A MEMO

SEND ME A MEMO

A Handbook of Model Memos

by

Dianna Booher

Facts On File Publications
460 Park Avenue South
New York, New York 10016

All names in this book are fictitious, and any mention of real people, products, companies, or places is merely coincidental.

LIBRARY OF CONGRESS CATALOGING IN PUBLICATION DATA
Booher, Dianna Daniels.
  Send me a memo.

  1. Memorandums.   I. Title.
HF5721.B63   1984   651.7′55   83-14058
ISBN 0-87196-906-8

Printed in the United States of America

10 9 8 7 6 5 4 3 2 1

CONTENTS

SEND ME A MEMO

INTRODUCTION

"Didn't you read my memo?"
> "Yes, I know what you *said,* but I didn't know that you meant . . . ."

"I didn't know her memo required a response."
> "It doesn't. This one is just for the files—call it self-preservation."

"I thought he only said, 'watch expenses.' "
> "He did, but 'watch expenses' in his vernacular means 'pick up paper clips.' "

"Did you get a copy of the new procedure?"
> "I got a copy, all right. Now if I can only find an interpreter . . ."

"Here's something that just came in for you."
> "Another memo from Burton? I should get through it by next December—maybe."

"You never did say who estimated this budget item."
> "Right, I had to omit that little detail for political reasons."

"Why don't you put it in a memo?"
> "Are you kidding? If I said what I'm really thinking, they'd fire me."

As the above comments suggest, memo writers don't always say what they mean and mean what they say. Nor should they. And those who do say exactly what they mean often wreak havoc with their career and/or business relationships. Others, paralyzed by fear and inadequate writing skills, struggle simply to get any words at all on paper.

Yet the business writer knows that his company places a premium on his ability to write clearly, concisely, accurately, quickly, and at times persuasively and diplomatically. To check yourself on each of these objectives, consider the following questions that may reveal trouble spots for you:

Clarity

Does your reader ever phone you about some memo detail "just to make sure"?

Are you frequently asked to define what you mean by certain words—for instance, "significant," "sensitive," "inadequate," "units," "unacceptable," "facilities"?

Do you find yourself having to send a follow-up memo to accomplish what you thought the first one would do?

Do readers question you about what you think you have already made perfectly understandable?

Conciseness _____

Do you have trouble keeping memos to a page or less?
Do you find yourself debating between too many or too few details?
Do you decide what you want to say *as* you write rather than *before* you write?
Do your readers often seem to miss key ideas?

Accuracy _____

Do you assume the typist rechecks figures, dates, or spellings that are questionable?
Do others point out exceptions to your generalizations?
Do others question your conclusions based on your stated facts?
Do you usually send out your first draft as final copy?

Speed _____

Do you waste time staring at a blank page, trying to get started?
Do you generally have to do more than two drafts of a memo?

Persuasion or Salesmanship _____

Do readers frequently feel manipulated rather than come around to your way of thinking of their own accord?
Do you frequently fail to get what you ask for—the contract, sale, transfer, raise, promotion, new responsibility, cooperation?

Diplomacy _____

Do people seem to get upset or balk at your requests?
Do you have trouble pointing out others' problems and errors and motivating them to make corrections?

Every *yes* answer above brings you face to face with the "bottom line" in business writing—money and image. First, consider the cost of:

- inaccurate orders and shipments
- accidents, injuries, and equipment failures due to unclear written procedures
- lost sales due to poorly written proposals

- research that is unnecessarily duplicated because the documentation of results was unclear or ignored
- time wasted on writing, revising, duplicating, reading, editing, and rewriting the same memo
- time wasted on follow-up phone calls for clarification of poorly written documents

In addition to time and money, consider the personal and company image conveyed by your writing. Whether a valid judgment or not, many readers will evaluate your job expertise by the memos leaving your desk. Your written word is documentation of your promotability.

In *People and Performance,* Peter Drucker writes, "The further away your job is from manual work, the larger the organization of which you are an employee, the more important it will be that you know how to convey your thoughts in writing and speaking. In the very large organization, whether it is the government, the large business corporation, or the Army, this ability to express yourself is perhaps the most important of all the skills you can possess. . . . This one basic skill is the ability to organize and express ideas in writing and in speaking."

Lest you argue that others don't really pay attention to bad writing, let me share some comments from my workshop participants about their colleagues' writing:

- "Jerry is the type who writes a two-page memo to tell me to turn out the lights."
- "A salesman from one of our branch offices writes me everything in one long sentence. You'd think you were reading a legal paper, where they join everything in dependent clauses to avoid loopholes."
- "My supervisor's not a native-English speaker, and when she edits my memos, she butchers them with stilted, stuffy phrases. But you can't tell her anything, because she's so defensive. I'm just grateful that I don't have to sign my name to what goes out."

Colleagues *do* notice your writing. What's more important to the company, if not to you personally, is that clients and the business community at large notice writing inadequacies and label your company's service or product accordingly. Company or personal image can be a fragile commodity; employees must handle even in-house writing with care.

With so many political considerations and so much time and money hinging on the results, people often freeze up when facing a writing project. You may be relieved, however, to learn that there is a formula you can plug new messages into without reinventing the format time after time.

The following five steps for effective writing present that formula first introduced in my earlier book *Would You Put That in Writing?* I suggest to my writing-workshop participants that they have the first three steps printed on their scratch pads, ready for drafting all memos:

Step One: Reader or readers—
1.
2.
3.

Step Two: Special problems anticipated in the
reader's reaction—
1.
2.

Step Three: Basic-format outline—

What's the message?

What action next?
Reader's
Mine

Details (These may or may not all be included, but
use this list to jog your memory about possible
omissions.)
Who?
When?
Where?
Why?
How?
How much?

Optional evidence to clarify

Scratch-pad outline for planning your memo message

Let me summarize these five steps that form the basis of the memo
models contained in the rest of this book.

STEP ONE: CONSIDER YOUR AUDIENCE FOR THE PROPER ANGLE

Good salespersons know the value of "slanting" their pitch to each prospective customer or client. If she is selling to someone who complains of always being behind in the department's work, the salesperson emphasizes the increased efficiency of the new equipment. If the customer is concerned with safety, the good salesperson talks safety features. Or if status seems to be the overriding interest, the salesperson paints the equipment as *the* status symbol of the modern, efficient office.

Likewise, an effective writer slants his memo message to fit his audience. How? Ask yourself the following questions:

Is there a single reader, or are there many readers? Not only should you consider whom a memo goes *to,* but also you must consider whom a memo goes *through.* Both the final recipient and the intermediary approver determine what you say and how you say it. Also, consider pass-on readership. How many people will get a copy of this communication to carry on their job or simply to stay up-to-date and informed?

Be specific about naming individuals or groups who will gather information from your memo. Certain people expect to see certain details; make sure they find what they need. Also, be sure to rank your readers in order of importance. The most important readers get their information first; lower-ranking readers get their details further into the memo.

What are the interests of your reader or readers? Top-management readers will be interested in the "big picture": Should we grant funding to the new project? How much money will this new operation save next year? Should we close down our manufacturing plant in Dallas? Do we need to develop a new security system? How should we take these actions? Who should do them?

Middle-management and general professional people will be interested in your overall message and specifically in how they fit into the "action" picture. How will their operations, structures, priorities, responsibilities, or budgets change because of your message? What decisions should they make or alter because of your message? How can they duplicate your results in their own department? Do you need their cooperation? In what way? Primarily these readers will focus on the *why* and *how* details of your memo.

Specialists such as auditors, geologists, data processors, or trainers will be interested in even more specific details: How deep did you drill the well? Should someone invoice for the equipment immediately? Which consultant should design the new sales course? What qualifications should be required?

Specialists need such details to carry out the objectives of the "big picture" message.

How will the reader use this information? To determine what details to include in your memo, ask yourself why this reader will want to know what you have to say. Will she make a decision based on the facts presented? Will she build on your records, research, or opinion and incorporate the information into a larger project? Will she simply follow your procedures to audit her accounts?

How much does the reader already know about the subject? Never repeat back to the reader what he has already told you. Neither do you need to spend time telling him the obvious. What educational background or experience does the reader have? How up-to-date is he on this policy, product, procedure, problem, or situation? When's the last time you've spoken or written to this person about the subject? The answers to these questions tell you how much detail you need to give and what technical terms or abbreviations you can or cannot assume the reader will understand.

STEP TWO: ANTICIPATE SPECIAL PROBLEMS IN THE READER'S REACTION

Needless to say, every person who sees one of your memos is not going to be thrilled with your message, and for good reason. On occasion you will have to bear bad news. Specifically, you can anticipate a special problem when your message does one of the following: Will you create extra work for someone? Will someone have to lose face to accept what you say? Will someone tend to procrastinate about the due date for the information or action you're requesting? Are you pointing out someone's mistake? If several people have input to a particular decision, do you hold the minority opinion? Will others be skeptical? Do you want to take responsibility away from someone? Will you yourself look incompetent as a result of your message?

If any of the above is the case, then you have to plan how to minimize an unfavorable reaction by tactful wording or whatever means you can devise to overcome the obstacle. Of course, you can never eliminate all personality, situational, or political problems that result from your message. But consider them beforehand and attempt to handle them in the most effective way.

STEP THREE: OUTLINE YOUR MESSAGE FUNCTIONALLY

People who would never dream of building a house without a blueprint often try to write a memo without even a thumbnail sketch of what they want to say; without forethought, their hand mysteriously inscribes words on paper, or their voice warbles into the Dictaphone.

When I ask workshop participants how many write two or more drafts of a memo, letter, or report, invariably everyone in the room raises a hand. Why? Few outline. Rather, they decide what they want to say as they write. Therefore, they have to get to the end of the memo before they figure out what they want to say. Once they've "discovered" their real message, then they must go back and write the second draft. What a waste of time and effort! That's like setting all the ingredients in the kitchen pantry out on the cabinet before deciding which kind of cake to bake.

What's worse, some writers never decide "what kind of cake to bake"; they merely set out the details in their memo and then wait for the reader to interpret the meaning and draw conclusions for himself.

To avoid this lackadaisical effort at writing, outline.

But let me clarify at the outset, I don't necessarily mean outlining as you learned in school—Roman numerals I, II, III, A, B, C, etc. Rather, outline functionally; use as many or as few words as you need, and organize the information into the order the reader needs it. For the most part, that means you will avoid outlining your ideas in the traditional academic format.

Nor will you use the traditional business format:

- Introduction—history of the situation or problem, instructions, re-statement of the question investigated
- Discussion (Body; Justification)—methods, tests, scope, exceptions, details and elaborations, summaries of past conversations and/or correspondence on the subject
- Conclusions and Recommendations—test results, consequences, changes to be made, overall costs, who should do what
- Attachments (Appendix)—tables, charts, forms, questionnaires, maps, contracts, previous correspondence, invoices

What's the problem with this traditional format?

First, the introduction generally consists of information already known to the reader. In many cases, the writer merely repeats back to the supervisor-reader what the supervisor-reader has told him in the first place. Such repetition wastes both writing and reading time. Even more dangerous, the reader may skim the first sentence or two, decide that he already knows what you're saying, and throw the memo aside, unaware that you give new information further into the document.

Second, the discussion section of the traditional format contains details that lead nowhere for the reader. She doesn't know which details are important or how these details fit into the action she may later be expected to take. For the most part, the details strike her as a random list of ideas, with little rhyme, reason, or relationship.

Third and most important, conclusions and recommendations delayed until the end cause a reader to muddle all the way through the memo as if blindfolded. The details make sense only after the conclusion or "bottom line" message has been stated. Nine times out of ten, the reader will have to reread the details after he knows what you're driving at.

Therefore, writing a memo in the traditional ascending format wastes a reader's time and obscures the significance of details. You, the writer, control his time and his comprehension by your organization.

This ascending format is useful in fiction writing, in joke telling, and occasionally in selling. The writer purposefully sets the atmosphere, paints the background, and lays the foundation to create suspense, to build interest, or to entertain.

But in most business writing, the first priority is to express a message—to give the reader the most important information in the fewest possible words. A business reader should be able to read the memos that cross his desk in the same way he reads the daily newspaper. He reads the informative, capsule headline. If he wants to know more, he reads the first paragraph or two. If he wants still more elaboration, he continues to read the article's details. As soon as his curiosity is satisfied, he may stop reading and know that he has not missed anything significant.

Effective business writing, on most occasions, should follow this same newspaper format, the descending order:

Basic Functional Format

What's the message?	Narrow, one- to three-sentence summary of your "bottom-line" message
What action next?	What action do you plan to take? Or, what action do you want your reader to take based on the message you have just given?
Details: Who? When? Where? Why? How? How much?	Not all will be necessary for every memo; avoid mentioning the obvious. Usually, the *why* and *how* details will be the most significant and require elaboration. If the who, when, where, and why details can be stated briefly in the first two sections, don't repeat them here.

Optional evidence:	Mention any form, table, chart, diagram, or copy of former correspondence that you have attached to make the message and action clearer.

Let's examine each of these four sections more closely:

What's the message? After focusing on your specific reader or readers, as you did in Step 1, you should be able to summarize briefly the significant information for this audience. You can empathize with the reader's impatience about not getting this "bottom-line" message quickly if you've ever stood in a department-store customer-service line behind someone who returned merchandise in this rambling manner:

> Well, sir, my daughter and I were in the store the other afternoon— Monday, I think, or no, it was Tuesday—and I was on the way to take her to a birthday party and in a hurry. Well, we had already paid for some other things and checked out when I just happened to notice your advertisement in the display window for picture frames on sale. So I went on out to the car and sent my daughter back to the picture-frame aisle to pick up the frame and go through the checkout again. And I never looked in the bag until the next day, because the package was in the trunk and . . ."

On, and on, and on, and on. It's the epitome of restraint to keep from interrupting to say, "Just tell him you want a refund, lady."

Your reader feels the same impatience when you get into details before stating the overall message of interest.

What action next? When you intend to take action based on the message you have given, state it: Do you plan to schedule a follow-up meeting for next month? Will you choose vendors for the new food-service facility? Will your staff begin testing the new equipment in October? Will you correct your records as shown on the last invoice?

Or you may want action from the reader; if so, state what you expect. Do you want her to return the completed form by February 18? Do you want her to be more accurate doing safety inspections? Do you want her to approve your attendance at a computer-training program in Atlanta? Do you recommend that accounting procedures be changed to eliminate duplication of effort? Should she begin marketing the new widget by the end of the year?

Sometimes the message *is* the action, and this section and the first become one. And occasionally, you send a message only to inform. If that's the case, make sure your reader knows no action is required.

Details: Who? When? Where? Why? How? How Much? After the reader has "the big picture" and knows what you plan to do or what you expect him to do, then he can read the details with understanding and purpose.

Of course, if the idea regarding *who, when, where, why, how,* or *how*

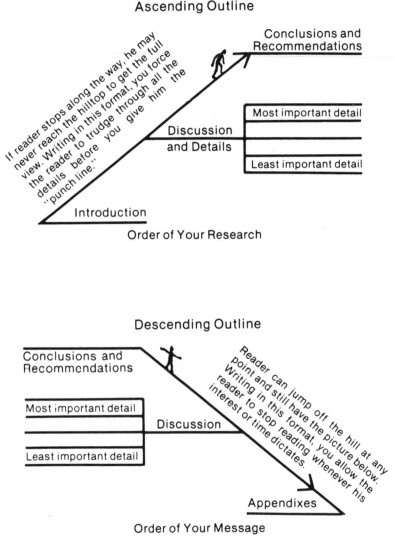

Ascending Outline

Conclusions and
Recommendations

Most important detail

Discussion
and Details

Least important detail

If reader stops along the way, he may never reach the hilltop to get the full view. Writing in this format, you force the reader to trudge through all the details before you give him the "punch line."

Introduction

Order of Your Research

Descending Outline

Conclusions and
Recommendations

Most important detail

Discussion

Least important detail

Reader can jump off the hill at any point and still have the picture below. Writing in this format, you allow the reader to stop reading whenever his interest or time dictates.

Appendixes

Order of Your Message

much can be given in only a word or a phrase, you will probably have already stated such information in the opening-message sentence or sentences:

> Department liaison persons helping to plan the headquarters move to 2011 Mainstay are scheduled to attend a meeting Tuesday, July 6, at 9:30 a.m. in Conference Room 203. Doug Pharmon will explain packing procedures and answer questions pertaining to your particular departmental equipment and files.

In this case, all pertinent details become a significant part of the message statement; you can give them briefly without elaboration.

In general, this third section of your memo contains those details that need elaboration—usually about *why* and *how*. If you anticipate a special problem in the reader's reaction, here is where you address that problem. If you expect skepticism, add authority to your position by elaborating on how thorough your investigation has been. If you expect hesitancy about a due date, impress upon the reader the importance of meeting the deadline. If you have claimed that a new procedure will save the company $80,000 next year, give the *how* of your calculations. If you must point out someone's error, tactfully allow possible reasons the mistake may have occurred.

Optional evidence. Not always, of course, will you have attachments with your memos. But attachments can make your message clearer or the action you expect from your reader easier to do. If you're asking for monthly data, can you send your reader a sample format to follow? If you want her to note discrepancies in past and present years' vendor contracts, can you attach a copy of the old contract so that she doesn't have to go through her files to make the comparison? If you're asking replacement of a stolen expense-reimbursement check, can you enclose another copy of your earlier-submitted expense form?

To repeat, this descending arrangement saves time for the reader. At his discretion, he can stop reading as soon as he has all the desired information. Further, the message-first format aids in comprehension of the details and attachments. Finally, outlining in this format gives you, the writer, a straight path to follow, helping eliminate irrelevant, repetitious, and obvious details.

To better understand how this format applies to your specific writing tasks, examine the following pairs of memos. The first model in each pair has been organized in the traditional ascending format; the second model has been organized in the functional descending format.

Pair Number One

Ascending Format _____

Subject:	Records Committee Recommendations Regarding Vital-Records Protection

Reader says, "So? What did you draft a procedure manual for?"

> As a result of a vital-records protection "pilot survey" conducted in eight departments, the Records Committee has identified 48 vital records and numerous protection schedules and has drafted a procedure manual. (The draft is attached herewith.)

Reader says, "So?"

> Also, we solicited responses to a vital-records protection questionnaire completed by the managers of the eight departments participating in the pilot survey. (A summary of responses is attached herewith.)

Major message buried here

> In view of the relatively small out-of-pocket expenses involved to develop, implement, and operate a vital-records protection program (estimated costs attached herewith), our committee hereby recommends that LLT promptly undertake to develop and implement a vital-records protection program for all organizational units located in our Dallas offices. We recommend that this program follow the LLT policy manual governing records retention, dated March 29, 198-, and the control concepts we have incorporated into the <u>Vital-Records Protection Procedures Manual</u> drafted as a result of the above-mentioned pilot survey.

Descending Format

Subject: Records Committee Recommendations
Regarding Vital-Records Protection

Major message and action

> The Records Committee recommends that LLT promptly undertake to develop and implement a vital-records protection program for all organizational units located in our Dallas offices. We suggest that this program follow the guidelines outlined in the LLT policy manual governing records retention, dated March 29, 198-, and also those control concepts in our attached draft of a <u>Vital-Records Protection Procedures Manual.</u>

Details — how we gathered data

> This recommendation is based on a "pilot survey" conducted in eight departments, a survey that identified 48 vital records and numerous protection

More details { schedules. Also, we solicited responses to a questionnaire distributed to managers of the eight departments.

Optional evidence — reader's choice to examine { Attached is a summary of the questionnaire responses from the eight department managers, our draft of the procedure manual, and the estimated, relatively small out-of-pocket costs of the overall program.

Pair Number Two

Ascending Format _____

Subject: Technical Review Meeting

"So why are you sending this now?" { Attached for your review is the Technical Review Packet for the Vehicle Cost Analysis system.

"So? Am I supposed to attend?" { The Technical Review meeting has been scheduled for Thursday, July 13, at 10:00 a.m. in room 446, ninth floor, Burton Tower.

"Message? I must be scheduled to attend." { If any additional information is required or if any scheduling conflicts arise, please contact me.

Descending Format _____

Subject: Technical Review Meeting

Message upfront { You are scheduled to attend the Technical Review meeting for the Vehicle Cost Analysis system. The

Action + brief details { group will meet Thursday, July 13, at 10:00 a.m. in room 446, ninth floor, Burton Tower. If you have a schedule conflict, please contact me.

Attachment + explanation { The attached Technical Review Packet for the Vehicle Cost Analysis system is for your review before the meeting.

Pair Number Three

Ascending Format _____

Subject: Establishing Procedures for
Handling Credit Records

**Introduction—
reader already
knows this!**

Within the past several years Shotwell has
experienced unprecedented growth and
development. We are now a large manufacturing
company, and we are on our way to becoming a
giant one. The Controller Department plays an
inherent role in this growth and development.
Effective procedures for the handling of credit
records are an integral part of the Controller
Department's responsibilities.

**Buried message
of interest**

As coordinator of the subject objective, I am
requesting your assistance in satisfactorily
establishing procedures. It would be beneficial to

Requested action

me at this time for you to list and evaluate the
types of credits received by your group, the
potential magnitude of those credits, and the present
procedures for handling them. In addition, please
assign one person from your group who is
knowledgeable about these credits to assist me on
this project.

**Details—what
data to supply**

The types of credits should include the following:
return of goods to vendors, credit advices,
settlement of disputed items, partial payments, stop
payments on checks, return of cash advances from
operators. These credits should not be limited to
manufacturing operations.

**Details—
to whom, when,
where**

The results of the evaluation should be documented
and sent to me by April 15, 198-, along with the
name of the person assigned to assist me. Should
there be any questions, please contact me in Austin
at extension 902.

Descending Format _____

Subject: Establishing Procedures for
Handling Credit Records

"Bottom-line" message { As coordinator of the project to establish procedures for handling credit records, I am requesting your assistance in the task. Would you list and evaluate

Reader's action { the types of credits received by your group, the potential magnitude of those credits, and the present procedures for handling them? In addition, please assign one person from your group who is knowledgeable about these credits to assist me on this project.

Details — what data to supply { The types of credits should include the following: return of goods to vendors, credit advices, settlement of disputed items, partial payments, stop payments on checks, return of cash advances from operators. These credits should not be limited to manufacturing operations.

Details — to whom, when, where { The results of the evaluation should be documented and sent to me by April 15, 198-, along with the name of the person assigned to assist me. Should there be any questions, please contact me in Austin at extension 902.

Optional attachment to make work easier { Attached is a sample format that you may find useful in compiling the requested data.

Pair Number Four

Ascending Format

Subject: IDRT Disk-Space Shortage

"So what?" { Below is a listing of datasets for your department, along with their dates of last access:

PR	.Trofv	1/6/8-
PR	.Trofvnn	2/4/8-
PR	.PL378	2/6/8-
HS	.AD257S	4/6/8-

"Oh, I see." { The IDRT currently has a disk-space shortage. At present there are over 10,200 datasets or about

Buried action { 87,000 tracks of allocated space that have not been referenced in over 120 days. Would you please review these datasets and delete those that are no longer required?

We appreciate your assistance in freeing this space.

Descending Format _____

Subject: IDRT Disk-Space Shortage

Message { The IDRT currently has a disk-space shortage. At present there are over 10,200 datasets or about 87,000 tracks of allocated space that have not been referenced in over 120 days.

Action { Would you please review the following datasets for your area and delete those that are no longer required?

Details—reader knows why he's scanning them {

PR	.Trofv	1/6/8-
PR	.Trofvnn	2/4/8-
PR	.PL378	2/6/8-
HS	.AD257S	4/6/8-

We appreciate your assistance in freeing this space.

Pair Number Five

Ascending Format _____

Subject: Reference Check on Telephone Consultants

"Obviously — they want clients!" { The telephone consulting group of R. R. Rainwater and Associates is still very much interested in Brunton International's becoming one of their clients. After our discussion with John Harliburn

But reader wants to know what you found out. { and Joe Chintz, I have responded to your suggestion and researched some of their past consulting jobs.

Details — do others agree?

Suspense builds!

At Quintony Natural Gas Company, Shreveport, I talked to Bob Black, who verified that the system recommended by Harliburn and Chintz has saved them money and is doing a good job. They formerly had an operator-controlled system that was replaced by a "Caller 302" in July 198- at the consultants' suggestion. Currently they have 42 trunks and 234 stations and are quite pleased with the improvements of this new system. Mr. Black said that some of the older employees had difficulty in adjusting to the new system but that most of the problems have been worked out. In his opinion, John Harliburn and his associate work very well with the telephone company, and the installation and implementation of their new system went smoothly.

Details — well, this is two opinions.

Suspense builds!

I next talked to Sinclair-Fuller Companies in Austin; Charles Maddox there seemed very impressed with the quality of work Harliburn and Chintz did. He said John not only worked well with the phone company, but also was successful in getting a rebate from them on overpayments made back in 198-. The greatest improvement according to Maddox was in the telephone marketing section (with 28 phones), where the new system is not only less expensive but also more efficient.

Details — now that's three opinions. The check must have been positive.

Finally, Jess Lamb of Brayswood in San Antonio discussed their experiences with me. His comments about John Harliburn were similarly favorable. He did say the "Caller 302" system was the second one to be installed in San Antonio and that the phone company was not as experienced as it should have been, taking about four months to work out the bugs. Only a few of Brayswood's employees have not fully accepted this new system. Mr. Lamb commented that even though they were aware of other consultants in the area, they never seriously considered anyone other than R. R. Rainwater and Associates.

Finally, the message!

In conclusion, it would appear that R. R. Rainwater consultants have a good background in telephone communication systems and that they do a good job in meeting the needs of their clients: They replace older systems with "Caller 302s" on a regular basis;

they are successful in establishing the correct tariff and securing refunds if and when they are warranted; they fulfill their commitments within the estimated time frame.

Detail—we should be careful here.

Only one of the references I checked had a word of caution. Charles Maddox of Sinclair-Fuller Companies commented that the consultants may be a little weak in detail as far as documenting their work in writing. Maddox said that he finally handled the problem by doing all of the detail memorandum work himself, simply having the consultants check for validity and then initial. He added that his company may require much more documentation than other companies would find necessary.

Details—reader knew this from the meeting.

During the next year we expect headquarters to expend approximately $423,000 for telephone conversations outside the Lubbock area. To install this new communication system will require an expenditure of about $350,000. For Brunton

Obvious wrap-up statements. "And they lived happily ever after."

International to realize a savings on either of these costs--with or without consultant assistance-- everyone must be willing to give new ideas a chance. This system, once approved, will become an ongoing program; it will not end when the consultants' contract is completed.

Descending Format

Subject: Reference Check on Telephone Consultants

Summary message— answer to reader's question. He may stop reading here + have the "big picture."

Since our meeting with John Harliburn and Joe Chintz, I have checked three references given by R. R. Rainwater and Associates and have received highly favorable comments. They have a good background in telephone communication systems and do a good job in meeting their clients' needs. Specifically, they replace older systems with "Caller 302s" on a regular basis; they are successful in establishing the correct tariff and securing refunds if and when they are warranted; they fulfill their commitments within the estimated time frame.

Most important detail

Only one of the references, Charles Maddox of Sinclair-Fuller Companies, commented that the consultants may be a little weak in detail as far as documenting their work in writing. Maddox finally handled the problem by doing all the detail memorandum work himself, simply having the consultants check for validity and then initial. He added that his company may require much more documentation than other companies would find necessary.

Specific comments of the three client companies follow:

Details — elaboration on references' comments. The reader may or may not read them; the choice is his. Details must be here, however, to support your upfront conclusion + to document the check.

At Quintony Natural Gas Company, Shreveport, I talked to Bob Black, who verified that the system recommended by Harliburn and Chintz has saved them money and is doing a good job. They formerly had an operator-controlled system that was replaced by a "Caller 302" in July 198- at the consultants' suggestion. Currently they have 42 trunks and 234 stations and are quite pleased with the improvement of this new system. Mr. Black said that some of the older employees had difficulty in adjusting to the new system but that most of the problems have been worked out. In his opinion, John Harliburn and his associate work very well with the telephone company and the installation and implementation of their new system went smoothly.

Details

At Sinclair-Fuller Companies in Austin, I talked with Charles Maddox, who seemed very impressed with the quality of work Harliburn and Chintz did. He said John not only worked well with the phone company, but also was successful in getting a rebate from them on overpayments made back in 198-. The greatest improvement according to Maddox was in the telephone marketing section (with 28 phones), where the new system is not only less expensive but also more efficient. His only reservation was the detail work I noted above.

Details

Finally, Jess Lamb of Brayswood in San Antonio discussed their experiences with me. He said their "Caller 302" system was the second one to be installed in San Antonio and that the phone company was not as experienced as it should have

Details ⎰ been, taking about four months to work out the bugs. Only a few of Brayswood's employees have not fully accepted this new system. Mr. Lamb commented that even though they were aware of other consultants in the area, they never seriously considered anyone other than R. R. Rainwater and Associates.

If your memo involves complicated and numerous details, then you will have to do additional outlining within the framework of the basic format.

First, to expand the basic format, begin with a random list of ideas. On a scratch pad, jot down every detail to be included. You may use words, phrases, or complete sentences—whatever will later jog your memory about the information to be included. At this point, don't stop to differentiate among major points, minor points, or attachments. If the idea comes to mind, record it. Then when you have listed all the information to be included, your eyes can scan the list and begin to see relationships, categories, and major and minor ideas. With another color ink or pencil, draw lines and arrows to rearrange details into logical order.

You probably practice this random-to-logical listing every time you run errands. Your "things-to-do" list first reads: "suit at cleaners, shampoo, lettuce, tomatoes, cucumbers, deodorant, gift for Marilyn, mail check, sandpaper, nails, blue tie, lacquer, stamps." But before you leave home, those of you who are more organized will then rearrange the list by "stops"; others of you will do the same reorganization mentally as you shop.

cleaners—suit
post office—mail check, stamps
discount store—deodorant, shampoo
mall—gift for Marilyn, blue tie
grocery store—lettuce, tomatoes, cucumbers
hardware store—nails, sandpaper, lacquer

Now, of course, as you shop you may shift an item to another stop at the last minute, getting sandpaper at the discount store rather than at the hardware store. The same is true of your list of memo details. You may always find at the last minute that something fits better in another slot and move it. That's okay. The main idea is to start with the random list and to record ideas as fast as possible so as not to lose your train of thought and miss anything while your mind is flowing.

When you have everything captured on paper, you can begin to see good, better, and best arrangements. The random listing and rearranging take the place of that often written but unnecessary first draft. Why write an entire paragraph complete with transition and summary to encase an idea that you may delete or move in the final copy?

Even when you write a special-format memo—one that requires guidelines, such as telling someone "no" or requesting cooperation—the random-list technique still applies.

Finally, review your rearranged outline to see that it still follows the basic format: (1) message; (2) action—yours and/or reader's; (3) details; (4) optional evidence attached. Have you stayed with the main point of the communication for your specific audience? Have you given all necessary details for all readers to take the required action?

When tackling a lengthy project, after you've done your own outline, review it with your supervisor to see that he agrees with your writing plan. Does he support your conclusions and recommendations? Have you covered all the bases? Does he foresee any problems, political or otherwise, that would suggest careful wording of the memo message?

If you can avoid doing so, never write a complete draft of a lengthy memo before getting some kind of approval from your supervisor or colleagues on the project. Even professional writers get editorial approval on their article or book outlines before wasting time to write final copy that may be unacceptable. Your time is no less valuable.

Allow approximately 50 percent of your total writing time for these first three planning steps.

STEP FOUR: DEVELOP THE FIRST DRAFT

Collect and assemble data *before* you start writing. Otherwise you'll waste time on a stop-and-start project, held up each time you discover a missing piece of information. Keep complicated data on individual note cards, matching the information to your expanded outline with a penciled notation at the top of the card. (Long notations on single sheets are difficult to shuffle and rearrange.) Finally, you are ready to dictate or type your first draft. Either is faster than writing by longhand and allows you to capture a free-flowing, conversational style.

This fourth step is the easiest part of the writing process; you're simply attaching flesh to the skeleton outline. If you have planned well (following Steps 1, 2, and 3), this step will take about 25 percent of your total writing time.

STEP FIVE:
EDIT FOR CONTENT, GRAMMAR, CLARITY, CONCISENESS, AND STYLE

Always allow a cool-off period before you begin editing. Otherwise, you simply read what you think you wrote. You miss gaps in logic, fail to see missing or irrelevant details, overlook grammatical errors, and find conciseness and style too difficult to bother with in this last stretch of the task. To avoid these hazards, take a few hours' or days' break; then you can edit with an objective view.

This last step makes the difference between an effective memo and one that will be ignored or will require follow-up clarification. If done adequately, editing will require about 25 percent of your total writing time. Don't skimp.

For a full explanation of editing for content, grammar, clarity, conciseness, and style, refer to *Would You Put That in Writing?*, pages 50–133. The following, however, will serve as a brief checklist on such matters. Perhaps you'd also like to use this checklist when editing a subordinate's writing. You can simply note the flaws you find without time-consuming, face-to-face discussion. The writer, then, can refer to the earlier book for extra help with his specific weaknesses.

EDITING CHECKLIST

Content

☐ 1. The slant of your message should be appropriate to your reader's interests. Eliminate unnecessary details.

☐ 2. Proportion should match emphasis. The most important ideas get the most space; less important ideas get less space.

☐ 3. Check accuracy (dates, numbers, drawings) and completeness (examples to make generalizations more specific). Add authority by substantiating claims with data, expert opinion, surveys, or specific observation.

☐ 4. Retain first-choice words. For example, if you call a document a "contract," don't later refer to it as an "arrangement" and still later an "agreement." The reader may wonder if you're still talking about the original document.

☐ 5. Paragraph by idea and for eye appeal. A paragraph may be as short as a sentence, but no longer than about ten lines for business writing. Otherwise, the material looks too heavy to read, and comprehension drops.

☐ 6. Use *informative* headings and adequate white space. For headings, think of newspaper headlines rather than empty captions such as "Discussion." Specific headings aid the reader in skimming and relocating material. Allow adequate white space before and after headings to give the reader eye relief and to make the material seem less difficult.

Grammar

☐ 1. Do not dangle verbals. For example: *"Deciding to rescind the earlier estimate,* our *report* was updated to include $40,000 for new equipment." (The report did not decide.) Correct: *"Deciding to rescind our earlier estimate, we* have updated our report to include $40,000 for new equipment." (We decided.)

☐ 2. Do not write fragments for sentences. Word groups must have a subject and verb and express a complete thought to be a sentence. For example: "He decided not to audit the last ten contracts. Because of our previous objections about compliance." The last phrase is dependent on the first clause for its meaning; the two must be joined in the same sentence.

☐ 3. Use parallel structure. Equal ideas should be structured alike in the sentence—all verbal phrases, all prepositional phrases, all clauses, etc. Not: "The owner questioned the occupant's *lease intentions* and *the fact that the contract had been altered with ink markings.*" But: "The owner questioned the occupant's *lease intentions* and *ink alterations* of the contract." Both equal ideas here are noun phrases serving as direct objects of the verb "questioned."

☐ 4. Make pronouns agree in number with their antecedents. Not: "An authorized *person* must show that *they* have security clearance." But: "An authorized *person* must show that *he* has security clearance." Or, to avoid sexist language, use the plural throughout—"persons . . . they."

☐ 5. Make verbs agree with their subjects. Be particularly careful when choosing the verb to follow the pronouns "which" and "that." Make sure you know what "which" or "that" refers to in each sentence. For example: "This is one of the public-relations (functions that is) (functions, which are) underbudgeted." If you mean *one* function is underbudgeted, use "is" for the verb after "that." But if you mean all public-relations functions are underbudgeted, use a comma after "functions" and "are" for the verb after "which." The verb choice, in this case, carries the entire meaning of the sentence.

☐ 6. Do not change tenses and moods unnecessarily. For instance, if you are giving procedures in the present tense and then carelessly use a past-tense verb, that particular step sounds like something apart from the procedure, something done previously. Or, if when writing instructions in the past tense you slip into the present tense, you sound as though you have stopped the procedure and are merely giving an explanation of what happens at this stage in the process.

☐ 7. Punctuate correctly. Use commas after introductory words, phrases, and clauses; between items in a series or independent clauses joined by *and, but, for, nor, so, yet, or;* before and after (to enclose) nonessential information. With longer connective adverbs such as *however, consequently, subsequently, therefore,* or *hence* between clauses, join the clauses with a semicolon. Not: "He did not make repairs, however, he continued to monitor the equipment." But: "He did not make repairs; however, he continued to monitor the equipment."
Also, use a semicolon to separate items in a series when the items already have internal commas. For example, examine the second sentence in the previous paragraph.

☐ 8. Choose appropriate words and phrases. Make sure you know the difference between words such as "affect" and "effect" and "operative" and "operational."

☐ 9. Spell correctly. Check the dictionary, particularly for hyphenation. Also, be careful about omitting apostrophes that show possession.

☐ 10. Do not clutter with capitalization. Capitalize proper nouns (and their derivatives and abbreviations), the first word and all key words in titles, and first words in sentences. If you intend to emphasize, underline or italicize rather than capitalize.

Clarity

☐ 1. Consider readability. Business communication designed for a college-educated audience should be written at the tenth- to twelfth-grade reading level. Prefer short sentences (averaging 15 to 20 words) and simple words. If you must use difficult, technical words, compensate with even shorter sentences than usual.

☐ 2. Position to indicate emphasis. The most significant ideas should come at the beginning of a memo or paragraph. But in a sentence, the position of most prominence is at the end. For example: "Because he was unable to attend the meeting personally, *he forwarded his congratulations on cassette tape.*" (Emphasis falls on his sending the cassette tape.) "He forwarded his congratulations on cassette tape *because he was unable to attend the meeting personally.*" (Emphasis falls on *why* he sent the tape.)

☐ 3. Link to show proper relationships. Make sure when you join two ideas in a sentence with "and" that both ideas are equal in importance. Subordinate minor ideas by placing them in the minor clause or phrase; elevate major ideas by placing them in the major clause.

☐ 4. Use clear transitions between ideas. Signal the reader where you're leading with cue words and phrases such as *but* (to contradict), *therefore* (to conclude), *also* (to add), *for example* (to illustrate). Repetition of a key idea or phrase can also serve as an effective transition.

☐ 5. Use clear references. Avoid beginning a sentence or clause with pronouns such as *this, that, it, they,* or *which* when there is more than one meaning for that pronoun implied in the previous statement. "These decisions have been a big disappointment to the committee members. They have delayed further action." Who or what are "they"? Decisions or committee members?

☐ 6. Place modifiers correctly. Place words, phrases, and clauses as close to the nouns they modify as possible. Particularly watch the modifier "only." "There are some discrepancies in several of the invoices that we are checking." Are they checking the discrepancies or all invoices? Not: "He could *only* reimburse the cost after July 15." But: "He could reimburse the cost *only* after July 15."

☐ 7. Prefer concrete words and phrases over vague, general ones. Don't say, "Our figures show a significant increase." What's "significant"? Instead say, "Our figures show an increase of 19%."

☐ 8. Use a consistent viewpoint. Especially when giving instructions, keep one reader in mind and give steps of action from his perspective. Avoid passive-voice verbs that tend to leave out who does what. Not: "Partial data should be submitted by April." But: "You should submit (or all data processors should submit) partial data by April."

Conciseness

☐ 1. Prefer active-voice verbs; make the doer of the action the subject of the sentence. Not: "It has been concluded that . . ." (5 words) But: "We conclude . . ." (2 words)

☐ 2. Dig buried verbs out of noun phrases. Not: "This arrangement *provides for the elimination of* costly repairs." But: "This arrangement eliminates costly repairs."

☐ 3. Avoid adjective and adverb clutter. Adjectives and adverbs (words of opinion) weaken the impact of a message. For example: "This project will *probably* be completed in a *few* days." "Probably" and "few" hedge. Be emphatic and to the point: "This project will be completed by Friday."

☐ 4. Cut cliches, redundancies, and little-word padding.

Style

☐ 1. Vary sentence patterns and length. Avoid the monotony of all subject-verb-object constructions. For variety, follow lengthy sentences with short ones.

☐ 2. Revise weak verbs. Substitute stronger verbs, particularly for forms of "to be"—*was, were, is, are*. When you use a weak verb, you then need adjectives and adverbs to add to its meaning. Not: "Brunton products are highly effective in . . ." But: "Brunton products excel in . . ."

☐ 3. Prefer a personal, conversational tone. Use pronouns and the active voice, keeping people in your writing. Not: "This information will be sincerely appreciated." But: "We sincerely appreciate your information." For the most part, write in your "talking voice"—flowing, natural, warm—being careful to eliminate grammatical errors, colloquialisms, and repetitions in the written memo.

As I stated earlier, these five steps apply to any writing project—from meeting announcements to procedures to technical proposals.

Models in the remainder of the book will serve to emphasize the basic format outlined in Step 3 by showing you how the format outlined in Step 3 applies to specific subjects. Also, the model memos include "special" arrangements for sensitive subjects.

Following each model is a list of do's and don'ts. These lists call attention to special considerations when you are writing for more than one reader or anticipating special problems in audience reaction.

Some categories have been included not because writers tend to make common mistakes but because their subjects are unfamiliar or infrequently handled. Models in these categories (such as sympathy or congratulatory notes) will save you time in developing specific content and wording.

THE MEMOS

ACCOMPLISHMENTS, TO DOCUMENT

Good Models

Subject: Cost Reduction in Utilities

During my May 6 discussion with consultant Herb Williams about our completed Harlin project, I discovered that Brewer Power and Light Company had erroneously charged us sales tax each month for electricity. Rules 21521 and 12528 of the Texas Sales, Receipts, and Use Tax Regulations exempt from sales tax electricity and gas used predominately for manufacturing.

As a result, I have instructed Jim Hart to request a refund of $26,005.23 in sales-tax payments by our division for last year. In the future we expect to save approximately $2,000 per month as a result of this exemption.

◆ ◆ ◆

Subject: Improved AFE Procedures

I'd like to suggest two improvements in the company's procedures for Authorization for Expenditures (AFEs):
1. Procedures should require that AFEs be closed within ten days after activity has ceased or by a specified date each month.
2. Accounting should confirm in writing that funds are available to be committed to an approved AFE.

These improvements will ensure that the accounting for costs is completed and that previously committed funds are released. Also, timely closing will improve accuracy of the records, because all parties will still be available to answer unresolved questions. Second, the Accounting Department's written confirmation (possibly through an additional signature line on the AFE form) will communicate to management that funds are available. Written confirmation will also alert Accounting to begin to accumulate contracts so that invoices can be speedily processed.

Ultimately, this procedure should prevent budget overruns.

◆ ◆ ◆

Subject: Accomplishments, July-December 198-

During the last six months of 198-, I have completed the following projects:

> Accounts payable: Accounts payable and the outstanding voucher listing have been reconciled to zero. This is the first such reconciliation since the system has been in operation.
> Accounts analysis: All account analyses have been completed and reviewed in conjunction with the closing of corporate books.
> Corporate monthly expense distribution: I have and will continue to approve all the account distribution of corporate expenses (comparing actual to budgeted expenses). This approval has reduced coding errors and improved the accuracy of our reports to management.
> Expense report procedures: New procedures have been approved and will go into effect April 1. We estimate a savings of four work days per month and increased accuracy in reporting travel-related expenses.

I look forward to making even more significant contributions to Allied in the next year. Thank you for your leadership and cooperation.

◆ ◆ ◆

Subject: Skills and Training Received with Bentco

Bentco has made a significant contribution this past year in upgrading my knowledge, skills, and training in both the library and the Systems Analysis Department:

Skills/Experience
* Increased typing skills from 50 to 70 wpm
* Set up and maintained filing system in the library
* Learned "Task List" and "Big Print" applications of the ROG system

Training Courses
* Verbal Communications
* Business Writing Workshop
* Secretarial Systems Seminar

Thank you for the opportunity to improve my skills and to learn more about the company's objectives. I look forward to a challenging career with Bentco as I formulate goals for this coming year and take on more responsibility in the Systems Analysis Department.

Do's

● Use the basic functional format, describing the essence of your contributions to the company, or the training and skills acquired at the company's or your own expense. If you have several accomplishments to document, make each topic a "mini-format"—message, action, details. (See the third memo.)

• Interpret the significance of your accomplishments: Is this the first such achievement? Has this new training prepared you for specific new assignments or promotions? If so, which ones? Will this skill or idea save money? How much? Does this idea, discovery, program, or procedure have other applications that can be investigated further for use in other departments? Never take for granted that your reader will "interpret" the significance of your contribution or training and reward you accordingly.

• Be modest, yet confident in tone. Note particularly in the last model that the writer's accomplishments are primarily acquired skills or training; accordingly, she has worded the facts in an appreciative tone. Also, rather than repeatedly using "I" in mentioning your activities, you may use the passive voice for the sake of modesty: "Accounts payable have been reconciled" rather than "I have reconciled accounts payable."

• Mention dates, where appropriate, to prevent someone else from claiming credit for your discovery or suggestion at a later time.

• If you have several accomplishments to mention, use informative headings and lists for the reader's easy skimming and recall. You want her to be able to get the "big picture" at a glance.

APOLOGIES

Weak Model

Subject: Data for the Blair-Rexton Project

I received your phone message last week about the figures I promised last month in Atlanta. I owe you an apology for not getting them to you sooner. Although you and I haven't worked together before, let me assure you that this is not my usual manner in handling things.

Please find the charts with the figures enclosed. They are rather self-explanatory; but if you have further questions, please do not hesitate to let me know.

I trust that this has not inconvenienced you irreparably in proceeding with your Blair-Rexton Project.

Don'ts _____

   • Don't gloss over your responsibility for the error, problem, or situation. If the situation is important enough for the other person to mention, it's important enough for a sincere apology. The writer here sounds unconvinced about the seriousness of the delay: "I owe you an apology . . ."; "I trust that this has not inconvenienced you irreparably . . . ." Notice that rather than humbling himself to say "I'm sorry," he has avoided that expression altogether. When you are at fault, admitting guilt disarms the reader and makes him much more willing to accept your apology and explanation charitably.
   • Don't remind the reader again at the end of your memo about the problem or disappointment. Instead, suggest that the matter has been corrected and that goodwill has been restored.

Good Model

Subject: Materials for the Supervisory Skills Course at Ridgemore Center

I have shipped your materials for the Supervisory Skills Course today by Express Mail; you will, of course, have them in hand before receiving this note.

Please accept my apology for the delay. Since everybody here in our office has observed the moratorium on spending, Doug Eddleman volunteered to load the box of manuals and cassettes on the company plane with him when he left for the meeting there on March 15. At the last minute, however, he became ill and could not attend the meeting. So naturally I panicked about the materials, as I am sure you did. I know how important it is for you as instructor to have the materials beforehand to preview, and I am sorry for what was poor judgment on my part.

Rest assured that I'll never "cut corners" in shipping your materials again. Thanks for your patience, and good luck with the course.

Do's

● Focus immediately on positive action taken to rectify the situation rather than recall the damage done by your error.

● Apologize with actions, not words. Is there something you can do to ease bad feelings? Take someone to lunch? Submit the next report a week early? Send over temporary typing help? Hand-carry the drawing to the client? Make a phone call to the vice president to assume your part in the problem and ease the strain on your reader? In other words, can you go the biblical second mile in salvaging the situation, relationship, or project?

● Briefly, in a positive way, explain how the mistake happened. Not to do so is inconsiderate. Let the reader know that your mistake was not intentional or due to unconcern.

● Make the reader feel that her goodwill is valued.

● Assure the reader that you will *guard* against future mistakes. (Avoid guaranteeing that something will never happen again. Murphy's Law will make you a liar, and then the reader will be doubly disappointed.) Mention that you are making a note on your calendar so you will not forget the next meeting; say that you have instructed your secretary to put future calls from the reader through to you immediately; promise that you will personally phone to follow up information you send in the future. Offer whatever assurance you can that the mistake will *likely* not recur. Note that in the previous memo the writer says he will never "cut corners" in shipping materials again; however, he does *not* promise that the materials will never be late or that the instructor will always have them when he needs them.

APPOINTMENTS, TO SET

Good Models

Subject: Request for Appointment about Career Plans

Would it be possible for you to see me if I drop by your office sometime Thursday or Friday afternoon? I'd like to follow up on our last month's conversation about my transfer into the public-relations field and about my selection of graduate courses next term. I do want to tailor my education to your objectives for me here at Perrington.

Please phone me at the Service Center (ext. 6897) to arrange a time convenient for you. Thanks so much for your interest in my career plans.

◆ ◆ ◆

Subject: Review of Records on the Binex Agreement

We have scheduled a review of your records associated with the Binex agreement for the week of March 19. If you plan to be out of the office or have other serious conflicts, please contact me at 223-4467 immediately.

Production allocation calculations, product pricing, and operating and maintenance expenditures for calendar year 198- will be reviewed as a "pilot" audit for accuracy and compliance with the contractual agreement. We expect to complete the review within two days.

APPOINTMENTS, TO CANCEL

Good Model

Subject: Cancellation of Budget-Controls Discussion

Bart, I need to cancel our budget-controls discussion scheduled for next Tuesday, June 16, in my office. Sometime next week, I'll phone to arrange another date to get together about this important matter.

I'm sorry for any inconvenience this cancellation may cause, but three key individuals from whom I need to gather information before you and I talk are on a field trip to our Oklahoma plant.

APPOINTMENTS, TO DELAY/REFUSE

Good Model

Subject: Requested Appointment about Zinc Oxides

In response to your request to meet and discuss new suppliers for our zinc oxides, I want to let you know that Bob Ageet is now handling our purchases of this product. Frankly, I haven't been involved with actual vendor decisions in the past nine months; therefore I can't intelligently respond to the price questions and delays you mentioned in your June 2 memo.

Please do feel free, however, to contact Bob about your concerns, and perhaps you and he can clear up any problems and consider new guidelines or controls. If after your discussions with Bob there is still some problem with the suppliers, please ask Bob to get in touch with me again.

Thank you for your attention to details such as this.

Do's

- State the scheduling, cancellation, or delay/refusal upfront.
- Always give some indication about the subject of the appointment when scheduling so that the reader can prepare beforehand any thoughts, data, or questions.
- Let the reader know if the appointment is mandatory or optional and how to contact you if there's a conflict.
- Give enough detail about the appointment date, time, subject, location, and duration when setting or canceling. Even with cancellations, this information prevents misunderstandings about exactly which meeting or appointment you are referring to.
- State any available information about rescheduling.
- Express concern for the other's inconvenience when canceling.
- Be sure to give reasons when delaying or refusing. If possible, point out why the appointment would not be beneficial to the requester or in the best interest of others concerned. Suggest alternatives for handling the problem, situation, or decision.
- If delaying or refusing an appointment, state any conditions under which you will reconsider your answer.

APPROVALS, TO REQUEST

Weak Models

Subject: High Plains Roadshow

As we discussed in Reno, we will be setting up this show the day before
the short training school in Tulsa begins. I believe this to be to our benefit.

As to the guest list, I would like to concentrate on the Carburetor Division
so that Ron Casper would be included on the invitation list. Also you may
want to invite Clamps and Couplings as we did last year? Maybe since we
are in a joint venture with Coursco Pipe, I should invite some of Bobby
McCall's customers. If we keep Bobby and his people at a low profile, we
should not get into any serious conflicts. I expect about ninety people from
High Plains, with only token representation from Tulsa. Another
consideration about the roadshow date is that this is the same night of a
scheduled and highly publicized political rally. However, I think we could
draw people from the rally over to the show. In fact, we could use the
political rally to promote the roadshow. Also, with your approval, I will be
inviting Ron Grimsley from the State Health Department as part of our
further attempt to get their attention.

Your thoughts?

◆ ◆ ◆

Subject: Beaumont Welding Center Addition, AFE 22-426

Preliminary plans for the Beaumont Welding Center office addition have
been reviewed with Bob Taylor and J. B. Hard. Both men feel that the
additional room should be large enough for three desk clerks. Additional
depth is needed for lockers and file cabinets.

The most practical size for this office would be an increase of depth from
10'6" to 12' and in length from 30' to 38', a total additional area of 140
square feet. The original estimate submitted in June was based on $102 per
square foot; therefore, the estimate needs to be increased by $14,280
(140' × $102). The budget figure may or may not have been increased for
inflation when it was carried over to the current year; but if inflation was
not considered, this would be the appropriate time to correct the budgeted
amount. Based on a 10 percent inflation rate since the estimate was first
made, the new budget figure should be changed to $107,600. Should I
proceed?

Don'ts

- Don't ramble. Even in an informal memo such as the first "roadshow" model, think before you begin writing and arrange related ideas beforehand, not as you write.
- Don't keep your reader in suspense about your request for approval. Notice that in the models above, the question of approval doesn't appear until the very end—"Your thoughts?" and "Should I proceed?" All the way through the details, the reader is wondering what the point of your communication is.
- Don't obscure the *exact* item or action for which you want approval.
- Don't bury significant details upon which the reader will make a decision. In the first memo, the total guest count is buried. In the second memo, the cost is buried. Most likely, approval hinges on these two key facts.

Good Models

Subject: Request for Approval for High Plains Roadshow Date and Guest List

After our discussion in Reno, I have given further thought to a date for the High Plains Roadshow and to the guest list. With your approval, I'd like to set May 23 as the date and invite approximately 90 people, including the following:

- * Carburetor Division (Ron Casper included here)
- * Clamps and Couplings Division (invited last year)
- * Coursco Pipe (customers of Bobby McCall's)
- * Ron Grimsley (from State Health Department, to further our attempts to get their attention)

Overall, I expect a good crowd from High Plains and only token representation from Tulsa. Although there is a scheduled and highly publicized political rally in High Plains on this same night, I think we can use the rally to promote the roadshow and draw people from it.

Your thoughts on the date and the above guest list?

◆ ◆ ◆

Subject: Beaumont Welding Center Addition, AFE 22-426—Request for Approval on Additional Space

After reviewing preliminary plans for the Beaumont Welding Center addition, Bob Taylor and J. B. Hard think the additional space should be increased by 140 square feet. This additional space (including an adjustment for a 10 percent inflation rate on the first estimate) will increase the total budget item to $107,600.

Do I have your approval to proceed?

This additional space will allow room for three desk clerks, lockers, and file cabinets. The most practical size would be to increase the depth from 10'6" to 12' and the length from 30' to 38', a total of 140 square feet. The original estimate submitted in June was based on $102 per square foot; therefore, the estimate needs to be increased by $14,280 (140' × $102), plus the 10 percent inflation rate on the entire project.

Do's

- State upfront exactly what you want approval for—in these models, date and guest list or increased expenditure. If you're not specific, the reader may simply rehash your ideas on one or any of your requests without giving a final answer.
- Use the subject line to indicate that the memo is a request for approval. Otherwise the reader may assume your message is only a progress report and delay reading it.
- Include all details your reader will need to make the approval decision. In the first model, that means total guest count and possible schedule conflicts that the reader may or may not consider acceptable. In the second model, significant details include use for the space and increase for inflation. Note that in the roadshow memo, the list of details (rather than paragraph format) makes each detail stand out in more readable form.

APPROVALS, TO GRANT

Weak Model

Subject: High Plains Roadshow

Yes, I think we should invite the Clamps and Couplings Division by all means; since they were included last year, omission this year would seem like a slight. Also, you are right about inviting Bobby McCall's customers at Coursco Pipe. Simply make sure we don't highlight their attendance from the microphone. Also, we should include Bill Wyatt's staff at Eastern.

It's too bad about the conflicting political rally on the night of May 23. But this date does seem to be our best alternative, since we do have to plan around the training school in Tulsa the following day. Anything later into the summer months would find too many key people out of the office on vacation. We have never tried anything as early as January or February, but building attendance would be difficult when the new-year workload is heaviest.

Keep up the good work; I'll look forward to hearing that the show was a success.

Don'ts

● Don't ramble into the details or reasons before stating that you are or are not granting approval. The reader's main interest is a "yes" or a "no." After she has her answer, she can better concentrate on your details, exceptions, or other elaborations.

● Don't be wishy-washy in your wording. In the second paragraph of the memo above, the phrase "this date does seem to be our best alternative" and then the "wondering" about a January or February date make the approval sound tentative. The reader must read between the lines for approval on the date.

Good Models

Subject: Approval for High Plains Roadshow Date and Guest List

The guest list and May 23 date for the High Plains Roadshow sound fine. Please do, however, add Bill Wyatt's staff at Eastern to your invitation list.

Keep up the good work; I'll look forward to hearing that the show was a success.

◆ ◆ ◆

Subject: Approval for Beaumont Welding Center Additional Space, AFE 22-426

You have my approval on the extra 140 square feet at the Beaumont Welding Center.

Do's

- Grant approval immediately. Also, use the subject line to clue your reader. Your approval is the basic message of interest.
- Omit all unnecessary details and repetition. When you say "yes" to the reader, she doesn't particularly care about your reasons for giving approval or agreeing. Only when you say "no" do you have to reinforce your decision with a discussion of reasons and circumstances. For a disapproval, refer to the " 'No' Replies" memo category in this book (p. 121).

AUDITS

Weak Model

Subject: Review of Investment Accounts of Cummings Company,
Cum-Helcro Company, and Comstock Company

Pursuant to the discussion Friday, February 2, 198-, review was made of
the investment accounts of the subject subsidiaries. Review was restricted
to determining if the investment account of each subsidiary properly
reflected capital contributions, equity in earnings, and partnership
distributions in each of the respective joint ventures. As of December 31,
198-, the combined investment in joint ventures for subject subsidiaries
was $88.4 million. None of the subsidiaries operates its respective joint
ventures.

The respective partner's equity reported in the Partnership Statement of
Partners Equity as of November 30, 198-, was agreed to the parent's
investment account as of December 31, 198-. This required a reconciliation
between the partner's investment account and the partnership's equity
statement, because the partnership financial statements are submitted a
month late and current-month activity is recorded based on estimates.

No discrepancies were disclosed in the review. Partnership transactions
have been properly recorded, and the respective investment accounts
appear to be fairly stated.

Don'ts

- Don't bury your findings. Information in the last paragraph of this
memo should come at the beginning of the memo so that the reader may stop
reading as soon as his interest is satisfied.
- Don't be overly formal. Audit messages are no more sacred than many
others. Formality has nothing to do with making the message "official." Don't
be afraid to use the active voice, personal pronouns, and a conversational
tone. Note the opening sentence above: "Pursuant to the discussion Friday,
February 2, 198-, review was made of the investment accounts of the subject
subsidiaries." Better: "After our discussion Friday, February 2, I reviewed
the investment account of the Cummings, Cum-Helcro, and Comstock subsidiaries."

Good Models

Subject: Billing of Investors

In auditing the January 198- billing, I noted that the investors had been correctly charged in accordance with the 198- Hite Exploration Agreement except for one area: Six trips totaling $1,833 for the first-level supervisor in the Production Department had been incorrectly charged to the investors. This charge should be made to the nonoperators.

I recommend that the prior months' billings be reviewed and that procedures be outlined to ensure that investors are charged as called for in the Hite Exploration Agreement. To correct the January billing errors, I recommend that adjustments be made in the following billing cycle.

◆ ◆ ◆

Subject: Audit of Approved Vendors List

Findings
At least 20 percent of the vendors currently used by Sedco are not on the approved vendors list as required by written procedures.

Recommendations
We recommend that the objectives and procedures of this vendor control be recommunicated to all involved individuals. Accounts Payable should compare invoices to the approved list and return invoices from unauthorized vendors to the appropriate manager for proper handling. The manager in charge must approve all additions to the vendors list. All departments should update their approved lists by September 30.

Background
Sedco's written procedure states: "Corporate business will be conducted only with vendors or contractors that are on Sedco's approved vendors and contractors list. Any additions to this list must be made by the appropriate manager."

The purpose of this control is to ensure that we are doing business with reputable, established vendors. Therefore, all departments should take care to see that their lists are updated and that decisions about additions to the list remain with the appropriate managers rather than first-level supervisors.

Do's

   ● Summarize the major message (compliance, noncompliance, discrepancies) upfront. Various accountants will then later examine details to carry out recommendations in their respective areas. For example, to have listed all invoices from unapproved vendors or names of vendors themselves upfront in the "Findings" section of the second model memo would have been inappropriate. If the memo were going to all departments, such a list, however, could be attached to provide a quick reference for each department to spot unapproved vendors with which it does business. The attachment, then, would not "clutter" the overriding summary message to the management reader.

• Use headings when appropriate. Headings guide multiple levels of readers to the sections of their interest. These headings become even more crucial in a lengthy discussion of findings and recommendations to be carried out in several accounting areas.

• Use a conversational style, not meaningless audit phrases that are ubiquitous in annual audit reports.

BIDS, TO INVITE

(Although bids go outside the company, they are included here because model-letter books make few, if any, references to them.)

Good Model

Dear Mr. Horowitz:

We would like to invite you to bid on the furniture requirements of Kilner, Inc., as specified on the attached list. Please forward your bid to me at the above address by February 13, 198-. If you have any questions in the bid's preparation, please phone me at ext. 3368.

The enclosed furniture specifications identify our exact company needs; please do not include in your quote any substitutions for items on the list.

Do's

- Use the basic functional format—message, action, details, attachment.
- Anticipate the special problem inherent in bids in that companies often quote for "in lieu of" items, making your comparisons of bids difficult. Either caution bidders against substitutions, or state that you will accept them.
- Make your specifications exact so that later you will not have to struggle with the apples-to-oranges comparisons.

COMMENDATIONS

Weak Model

Subject: Commendation on Time-Management Skills

From your March sales reports, I see that your new time-management skills have paid handsome dividends. Proper time management adds up to additional selling time, which means more closing opportunities, which, in turn, mean more sales. Overall, our team sales rose 38 percent during this month.

During our last meeting, I pointed out some of your trouble spots, such as random scheduling, delayed appointments, and paperwork. From your current reports, I see that on the average we made 1.6 more calls per day and all weekly paperwork has been submitted on schedule.

You learn quickly; I'll be expecting even greater things in April.

Don'ts

  • Don't sound manipulative. Let your intent be to congratulate on work well done rather than to motivate to greater achievement—although commendations often do have motivational effect.
  • Don't allude to your own part in the achievement. In this model, notice that the writer implies that his own tips were responsible for his salespersons' successes. The memo has an I-told-you-so ring.
  • Don't focus solely on benefits to the company to the exclusion of personal rewards. The writer of this memo would have done better to mention the average rise in *individual* commission or dollar sales or less *personal* after-hours time in preparing and submitting paperwork.

Good Models

Subject: Mounting Sales of XYZ Widgets

Ted Box has reported to me that you have been successful in selling seven XYZ widgets during February. My congratulations on this outstanding achievement.

I know that this kind of results takes a good deal of planning, time, and creativity to tailor your sales presentations to the specific customer's needs.

And your effort in attending the "closing" seminar in San Francisco, I'm sure, has certainly had much to do with your present success.

Please know that we recognize outstanding work such as this. My best personal regards.

◆　◆　◆

Subject:　Outstanding Job at the Oakland Data Center

Gene, you and your people have done an outstanding job in working together to solve the problems we encountered at the Oakland Data Center last year. I have had many comments from my customers lately on our improved reliability, customer services, and absence of critical problems. Universal Corporation has been especially complimentary about our services.

Special thanks to Joe Smartley, Lisa Henry, and Mary Johnson. Keep up the good work.

◆　◆　◆

Subject:　"Scheduling for Success" Campaign--Exceptional

Such enthusiasm as you have been able to generate in your staff in launching the "Scheduling for Success" campaign is contagious. You have taken us from the let-not-your-right-hand-know-what-your-left-hand-doeth state of affairs to an effective method of coordinating our publicity efforts.

And to top off the practical, the staff seems actually to understand the intricacies of the process; their own follow-up divisional campaigns suggest that they have really "bought into" your theory.

Rest assured that a bonus will be forthcoming later in the year. Until then, a 21-gun salute.

◆　◆　◆

Subject:　Twenty-five Years Service Award

I am pleased to enclose with this memo a Service Award Certificate to commemorate your twenty-five years of service with Benington's.

Our good reputation in the community is based upon the loyal commitment of our employees. In fact, in a recent phone conversation one of our few "complaining" customers remarked about your concerned efforts in righting our invoicing error. It seems that having you on staff was one of the few things in her estimation that we'd done right!

Along with this honorary recognition to display on your office wall, I thank you sincerely for your efforts on behalf of the company.

Best wishes for many more years with us.

Do's

- State the overall commendation first.
- Be specific in your praise; don't cloak your commendation in vague generalities that sound as though they came from a form letter or memo. Notice specifics in the preceding models: planning time and effort, shared customer comments, follow-up successes of subordinates.
- Be informal in tone; think of your memo as a warm handshake or the proverbial slap on the back.
- When you can, commend with tangible rewards such as bonuses, increased commissions, public recognition (with a distribution list), or even more responsibility. Never, however, promise what you can't deliver.
- Name names when commending a group. People, not departments or divisions, do the work. Make each feel that his or her individual contribution to the whole has been noted.

COMPLAINTS, LATERAL

Weak Model

Subject: Computerized Purchasing System

Your Mr. Tom Brown and Fred Smith visited me this week and wanted to know where I wanted two data-processing consoles installed. I had no idea what they were talking about, and yet they told me you had advised that we were to receive this equipment in March. I told them to forget about installation until I had been informed of what all this is about and what your intentions are.

On January 6 I sent a memo to your Mr. Ted Jones to confirm a meeting with him. Enclosed with the memo were our comments on the data printout form he was proposing. We received absolutely no response from him, nor have we had subsequent discussions of how our needs could be programmed.

Then on February 16, when we questioned the purpose of your requisition 1224-55 for contract programming services, we phoned your office again. We were assured that this invoice had nothing to do with our project but rather was for work done for the Indonesian group.

Frankly, John, I'm upset over this development. You have not kept me informed on progress nor advised me of your intentions.

Obviously, we do not plan to proceed with anything until we know what is involved, what is required, and why it is required. Frankly, we don't believe that computer programmers should decide what the user should have. I had assumed from our initial discussions that the development of a purchasing-system program would be a mutual task between us—not a unilateral decision from your end. Obviously, I was wrong.

Don'ts

 • Don't start with once-upon-a-time detail. The reader here cannot be sure of the exact nature of the complaint until the fourth paragraph above.
 • Don't omit detail about the *real* problem. The reader must have enough explanation to follow the developments and correct the situation. In this case, the reader still does not know where his programmers and the memo writer differ about computer needs: Is the actual program design inefficient for the Purchasing Department, or is the writer simply angry that he didn't have the proper input and notification? The person handling the complaint from this

point must read between the lines or pull the past memos and meeting minutes from the files to see which is the case.

• Don't fail to suggest how the problem can be remedied. In this case, the reader has no clearly outlined steps to follow to mend damage to the relationship or to the project.

• Don't use a self-righteous or aggressive tone. Note the "fight" words in this model: "Your Mr. Tom Brown and Fred Smith" and "your Mr. Ted Jones" (patronizing); "I had no idea what they were talking about" (exaggeration—of course he had some idea); "forget about installation" (hint of patronizing dismissal); "what your intentions are" (sound as if they are underhanded); "I'm upset . . . You have not kept me informed . . ." (personal attack); "Frankly, we don't believe that computer programmers should decide what the user should have" (assumes this is the reader's intention); "Obviously, I was wrong" (sarcastic, self-righteous statement of being wronged).

Good Models

Subject: Computerized Purchasing System

Frankly, John, I am dissatisfied with the development of our mutual project to computerize the purchasing system. I do not feel that my staff and I are up-to-date on the project or that we've had sufficient input about our specific needs. Therefore, I don't want to proceed with the plans until we talk further.

Could you, Tom Brown, and Fred Smith meet with me Thursday morning at eight in my office?

On January 6 after a meeting with Ted Jones, I enclosed in a memo to him our comments on the data printout form he was proposing. However, I've had no written response from him or subsequent discussions about how our needs can be programmed. Then on February 16, we noted and questioned the purpose of your requisition 1224-55 for contract programming services. I talked with Merle White by phone, and she assured me that this requisition had nothing to do with our project but rather was for work done for the Indonesian group. So, of course, when Tom Brown and Fred Smith visited me this week and wanted to know where I wanted two data-processing consoles installed, I asked them to wait until I had further discussions with you.

Attached are copies of the past correspondence so that you can easily follow the development of events.

I look forward to our meeting so we can get on with this project.

♦ ♦ ♦

Subject: Passing the Buck, er, Boxes

Help, I've got a problem. Would you lend a hand to a department and damsel in distress? We need the counter and cabinet space in the copier room that is now filled to overflowing with boxes of computer paper.

Our only consolation is that DP is using computer paper like Carter's Little Liver Pills. Ah, and even that provides only temporary relief before the little blue delivery truck unloads more boxes on our turf.

I spoke with John Ikeman about moving these boxes, who spoke with Fred Little, who spoke with Harold Smith, who at last mention had spoken with everybody except the Pope. All to no avail. According to all supervisors, their own storage space is occupied by things from outer space--or at least from someone else's department.

Any help you can provide to get other departments to remove their paper and supplies from our copier room (even trap doors may be a possibility) will be appreciated. Otherwise, the next time the little blue delivery truck pulls up, I may leave in a little white van.

Do's

- Let the reader know immediately what your exact complaint is.
- Suggest, even though you can't command, the action you want your reader to take to resolve the problem. Leaving correction to your reader's discretion increases the likelihood that the complaint will not be handled quickly and appropriately. If you have no suggestions, say so.
- Give enough detail so that the person stepping in to remedy the situation knows or recalls what has happened in the past. But be brief; avoid throwing in irrelevant details about how much trouble the situation has caused you—*unless* such detail is pertinent to correcting the problem or creates urgency. Always give names or dates involved and copies of past correspondence for the reader's convenience in following and verifying what you say. Notice that even in the last model above, the writer mentions people whom she's talked to but who were unable to correct the situation. By informing the reader of your previous action, you eliminate repetition of those nonsolutions.
- Use a conciliatory tone. First, that means not assuming that the harm or mistake has been intentional. Don't take away all your reader's possible "excuses" for the situation; allow him to save face. (There's no harm done in his saving face as long as the problem gets corrected.) Second, use "I messages" to minimize attack on the other person: "*I* do not feel that *my* staff and *I* are up-to-date on the project or that *we've* had sufficient input about our specific needs." Not: "*You* have not kept us up-to-date on the project, and *you* have not allowed us sufficient input about our specific needs." Also,

play down a self-righteous tone by active-voice rather than passive-voice constructions: "A problem has developed." Not: "You have created a problem."

• Show confidence that the complaint will be handled appropriately.

• End on a business-as-usual note. In the first model's concluding statement, the writer essentially says, "Let's get this worked out and move ahead." There's no "you're-on-my-blacklist" tone.

• Use humor when you can to attract attention to the problem and make the corrective action less arduous. Make sure, however, that you know your audience so that your humor is not offensive or does not make light of a situation others consider "no laughing matter."

COMPLAINTS, UPWARD

Good Models

Subject: Problem with Sunlight in Main Lobby

Our main-lobby receptionist is having a problem with the blinding sunlight streaming in through the windows above the revolving doors. On sunny days, she is unable to sit comfortably at her desk until midmorning or even later. In addition to her discomfort, visitors seated in the lobby have frequently commented on their discomfort.

I'd like to suggest that blinds be installed or that some kind of coating be applied to the window to cut the glare and to protect from the rays. If some solution is not found by the summer months, we will have to rearrange the lobby completely.

Please let me know on which solution you decide, and I'll handle the details.

◆ ◆ ◆

Subject: Priority and Follow-up on Maintenance Purchase Requisitions

A primary goal in Maintenance is to minimize downtime and to keep all equipment operational. To accomplish this goal successfully, we need help from Purchasing--priority treatment and confirmation of requisitions.

Out of approximately 300 requisitions I submit pcr month, only about 30 percent are confirmed. I realize, of course, that Purchasing has a tremendous work load and has difficulty distinguishing between emergency and "normal" orders. And, of course, I know that some of the replacement parts we order on short notice can't be confirmed. I do, however, try to keep these replacement parts in supply to avoid this rush situation. But nonconfirmation on other, standard requisitions has become a real problem in relation to productivity, downtime, and cost of repair and replacement parts via air freight.

Would you let Purchasing know of this problem and suggest that maintenance requisitions get first priority? Additionally, we'd like follow-up confirmations on promised shipping dates. I've attached a copy of our requisition log from 3/1/8- to 5/30/8- so that you can note which ones have not yet been confirmed.

Please let me know how these requisitions will be handled in the future.

Do's

● State the problem briefly as it relates to company profits and operations, if possible, rather than to your own inconvenience or wishes. In the first model, pointing out visitors' discomfort adds urgency to the situation. In the second model, the issue is keeping equipment operational, minimizing downtime, and avoiding unnecessary air-freight charges.

● Investigate and suggest solutions even though you do not have final authority. By this preliminary work, you increase your chances of getting a quick, appropriate response. Include all the details that the reader needs to take your suggested action.

● Assume your share of the blame when appropriate, or acknowledge the difficulty of the problem to be handled. In the last model, the writer acknowledges difficulty in confirming emergency orders. He also concedes that his orders for replacement parts cannot always be confirmed by Purchasing.

● Use a tone that shows confidence in a supervisor's positive response. In the second model, the writer tactfully implies that the Purchasing Department will cooperate if someone simply points out the problem. Avoid, however, sounding manipulative.

● Ask for a response. Otherwise, your reader may assume you're writing just "to get something off your chest" and/or "out in the open."

COMPLAINTS, DOWNWARD

Good Models

Subject: Speeding Up Loan Processing and Approval

When you send a loan request to us for approval, would you also send along a signed note and a copy of the board of directors' meeting minutes authorizing the loan request? This would certainly speed up the processing and approval here in our office.

◆ ◆ ◆

Subject: Petty Cash Disbursements

From the discrepancies between the actual balance in our petty cash box and the balance shown on the disbursement/accounting record, it is apparent that not all receipts are being returned and recorded.

To improve our petty-cash accounting procedures, Sherri Blunton (or in her absence Michaela Smith) will disperse all funds from the cash box. She, then, will be responsible for recording all withdrawals, collecting and recording receipt amounts, and noting returned cash.

Thanks for your cooperation in correcting this matter.

Do's _____

- Use the basic functional format.
- Avoid using the term "complaint" or "problem." Notice that the subject line in the first model highlights the motivation for resolving the matter rather than highlights the complaint. Simply because you have the necessary authority to complain and get immediate action, don't press the advantage. If you can get action with a whisper, why shout?
- Keep the tone positive, not sarcastic or overbearing. You do this by offering reasons for the complaint and directed action and by avoiding a personal attack on character or motives. Assume the problem is a matter of oversight in a situation where your message may be taken as an accusation of dishonesty or incompetence.
- Focus primarily on appropriate action or inaction, not blame and responsibility for the problem. Those under your supervision will generally be wary about any complaint from you and tend to read into it a "black mark" against their record. Such a "watched" feeling can prohibit a business-as-usual response on their part.

CONFIRMATIONS

Good Models

Subject: Natural Gas Regulation Course

This will confirm your registration for the Natural Gas Regulation course to be held at the Shamrock Hilton, March 3-4, 198- from 9:00 a.m. to 5:00 p.m. both days. If you must cancel, let us know immediately (ext. 4477).

In order for you to receive the most benefit from the course, we recommend that you review your course materials (attached) prior to attending the class.

The first workday after the course, please submit a completed "Training Evaluation Form" (also attached) and a brief summary commenting on benefits you derived, deficiencies in the course content, instructor's presentation, and meeting format. Feel free to suggest any improvements in any of these areas.

If you have other questions about the workshop preview assignment or evaluation, please ask.

◆ ◆ ◆

Subject: Confirmation of Future Career Plans

Thank you, Ms. Morton, for the chance to sit down with you last Friday afternoon and discuss my career objectives and contributions to Universal's training program. If I am correct, we have agreed on the following matters:
1. Within six months or less, my job title will be changed to Assistant to the Director of Employee Education.
2. My assignments will include all that I am now doing; additionally, I will be allowed to sit in on administrative meetings and voice ideas about curriculum plans.
3. My salary will be raised to $26,000 at the time I assume this new title.
4. I'll be given a car allowance of $75/month to cover trips to outlying centers.

If I'm correct about our agreement, would you sign this memo and return it to me for my files?

◆ ◆ ◆

Subject: Confirming Request for Company Plane

This memo is to confirm my phone request for the <u>Rising Star</u> on Monday, October 15, 198-. B. J. White, R. T. Bleyl, and M. K. Wilson will be flying to Atlanta to talk with Nelcro representatives about the delayed U1-terron Project.

We plan to depart the company hangar at 7:30 a.m. on Monday, October 15, and will leave Atlanta at 2:30 p.m. that same day.

If there is any conflict, please let me know immediately.

◆ ◆ ◆

Subject: Santa Theresa Exchange

We confirm that your memo of March 12, 198-, and the contract you enclosed with it are acceptable for our purposes on the Santa Theresa Exchange. We have forwarded our check for $88,000 to Boyton National Bank.

When you are ready to begin the final phase of this transaction, please give us five days' notice before forwarding the contracts.

Do's

- Use the basic functional format.
- Repeat *all* details of the appointment, course, meeting, speaking engagement, transaction, or whatever: date, time, place, enclosures, amounts. In short, don't rely on any previous oral or written information; repetition of details is one of the main purposes of the written confirmation.
- Mention the date or manner of any initial phone, personal, or written contact/agreement/meeting/request.
- Unless routine or obvious, suggest a method to contact you in case the confirmation note reveals some error or misunderstanding.

CONGRATULATIONS
(business and personal)

Weak Model

Subject: Article in <u>Science Today Journal</u>

Barney, I've read your article entitled "High Temperature Molecular Spectroscopy" that recently appeared in <u>Science Today Journal</u>. The editor's choice of title surprised me, though, because it did not really tell me the whole story of your paper. I was expecting to see more about the matrix isolation techniques.

Congratulations on publishing your work; I've got to find the time to get something into print myself before long. I've been working on a project that has possibilities and perhaps you can offer some tips when we get together later in the fall.

I'll be looking forward to hearing from you and again, congratulations.

Don'ts

- Don't imply that you or someone else could have earned the same honor or achieved the same results, given the same circumstances. The writer above hints that publishing is only a matter of time to write—time he simply hasn't had.
- Don't mention negatives—even negatives that have nothing to do with the congratulated person himself. The above comment about the editor's choice of article title dampens the overall message. Such comments, even though general or directed at other people or events, detract from the good feelings that the memo proposes to evoke on the part of the reader.
- Don't talk about yourself or the company; focus on the other person.

Good Models

Subject: Congratulations on Graduating Class Address

Congratulations on the honor of being asked to address the class of graduating seniors at Bellview College. (Tony Block sent me a copy of the graduation program.) To be singled out as one who could offer respected words of wisdom and inspiration on such an occasion is a noteworthy honor; especially when we recall the biblical lament about the prophet's reception in his own country. The occasion should give you much personal pride.

We appreciate your contribution on the company's behalf.

◆ ◆ ◆

Subject: Congratulations on Your Promotion

So you've finally arrived; Shirley Menitz tells me that you received notice yesterday of your promotion to hospital administrator. With your fund-raising efforts of last year and the overwhelming community support you've been able to generate, you may possibly be administering the best private medical care in the state. But I'll try to avoid having to check in to find out.

Warmest wishes.

◆ ◆ ◆

Subject: Do I Hear Wedding Bells?

We are all delighted to hear that you've finally taken the big step and plunged into unmitigated happiness; congratulations on your upcoming marriage to Suzanne.

Those of us who have worked with you the past two years say you deserve the best. We wish you many years of joy together.

◆ ◆ ◆

Subject: Congratulations on Your New Baby

We know that the birth of your son, Jeremy, was a very special event for you and your husband. I'm sure you are both quite proud. Congratulations to all three of you.

We wish for you wisdom in all those momentous decisions and situations that will be coming your way and also the best for Jeremy's health and happiness.

We'll be looking forward to photos soon.

◆ ◆ ◆

Subject: Birthday Wishes

According to my calendar, you've got a special day coming up January 14. This note brings wishes for a happy birthday and an adventurous, rewarding year to come.

Do's

• Mention the event or honor immediately. Don't keep the reader in suspense about your reason for writing.

• Be personal without being too familiar. Avoid general, stilted phrases that make the memo sound like a form message sent to all employees in the company. Inserting names rather than vague nouns like "your child" or "your new bride" will go far in personalizing your wishes. However, avoid familiarities such as mentioning age in a birthday wish, a past divorce in a wedding note, or a physical handicap in a congratulatory birth message.

• Be specific in your congratulations on achievements such as promotions or awards. The reader wants to know that you understand all that his achievement or honor entails—time, effort, creativity, intellectual accomplishment. Elaborating on these specifics gives the reader time to "enjoy" your attention.

• Be sincere. An effusive display of flattery makes even a great accomplishment seem small or undeserving of your notice.

COOPERATION, TO REQUEST

Weak Models

Subject: Written Communication

This division has a multitude of activities every day but obviously not enough written documentation of same! Word-of-mouth is the easiest but definitely not the safest means of communication.

Emphasize to your staff the need for file copies of important matters. On occasion, a handwritten note will be sufficient; at other times, an officially typed and signed letter is appropriate. Give individual guidance where necessary, and make sure "supervisors" understand! This is the second time around; eventually they'll catch on.

◆ ◆ ◆

Subject: Power Shutoffs

I hereby request that your men in Maintenance notify our geologists when the power is to be shut off to <u>any</u> part of our laboratory for <u>any</u> length of time.

Power shutoffs severely affect our research projects.

Don'ts _____

- Don't sound demanding. A reader will have an adverse reaction simply because the tone sounds like a complaint rather than a request for cooperation.
- Don't focus on the negative to the exclusion of the positive. In the first example, the writer could have pointed out the usefulness of having written procedures.
- Don't be too general in your requests. In the first memo, exactly what activities does the writer want documented in writing? Obviously he has in mind specifics that generated his request; some guidance is in order.
- Don't use underlining, unusual punctuation marks (such as an exclamation point), or quote marks when your message could be construed as a complaint. The quote marks around *supervisors* in the first memo make the word a sarcastic dig. The reader will hear you shout at underlining or exclamation points. Neither is appropriate with these requests.

Good Models

Subject: Necessity for More Documentation

Written documentation of our division's activities has been lax.
Word-of-mouth is the easiest but definitely not the safest means of
communication. In fact, at present we have an ongoing disagreement about
a rather large nonbudgeted expenditure that presumably was okayed by
telephone but not in writing.

For your own protection as well as for the smooth operation of our
division, please emphasize to your staff the importance of file copies
documenting agreements, approvals, directions, solutions to problems,
minutes of meetings, reprimands, and other such matters. On occasion, a
handwritten note will be sufficient; at other times, an officially typed and
signed letter is appropriate. Please give individual guidance to your
supervisors to make sure they understand when documentation is
necessary.

Thank you for your help to "put it in writing."

◆ ◆ ◆

Subject: Power Shutoffs

Could you please have your maintenance staff notify our geologists when
the power is to be shut off to any part of our laboratory for any length of
time? Since power shortages of even a few seconds severely affect our
research projects, we need this information in advance to prevent loss of
both time and dollars.

This request for advance notification, of course, is in no way an attempt to
regulate the work schedule of your men, but simply a request for improved
communication between our departments.

Thanks for the consideration you have given us in the past.

◆ ◆ ◆

Subject: The Auditors Are Coming!

From April 23 through May 4, the Durham auditing team will return to do
a full accounting audit of First City. They will be checking balancing
procedures, approvals, documentation, and tickler files as they apply to

each of our departments--Loans, Credits, New Accounts, Bookkeeping, Operations, and Security.

Let's strive for excellence in every area. You can do it!

♦ ♦ ♦

Subject: Flag, Motherhood, Apple Pie, and the Monthly Report-- Accuracy, Timeliness

The monthly ERT report has become the number-one financial report in all of Newmell, Inc., having attained a prominence that ranks right in there with the flag, motherhood, and apple pie. In fact, it's management's single best tool for planning and, therefore, deserves top priority in timeliness and accuracy.

I've enclosed a poster that well depicts the report's importance; please display it on a wall in your department or over the desk of the person responsible for getting this report to me each month. With this reminder, I encourage you to give the ERT your finest efforts.

Thanks. (Apple pie is coming under separate cover.)

Do's

- State the problem and/or request immediately.
- Find positive motivators. Point out the benefits of cooperation to your reader—smoother operations, safety, savings in time and dollars, commendation, or simply goodwill.
- Give reasons for your request. Not to do so seems arbitrary. Parents may not always give children reasons for their orders, but adults owe that courtesy to other adults.
- Be specific about requests. Note that in the revised "documentation" memo, the writer mentions exactly what activities he wants in writing—agreements, approvals, directions, solutions to problems, minutes of meetings, and reprimands.
- Anticipate and tactfully handle any negative reactions you expect. Notice that in the second memo, the writer assures the maintenance supervisor that his geologists will not try to tell his maintenance men when they can or cannot turn off the electricity.
- Emphasize important details by putting them in a separate sentence or paragraph or by repeating them rather than underlining, capitalizing, or punctuating for attention.
- Include courtesy words. Soften commands with words and phrases such as "we would appreciate. . . ," "would you please. . . ," "thank you for. . . ."

● End on a positive note. Assume your reader will comply. Either express gratitude or show confidence in the desired outcome rather than referring again to the situation as a problem.

● Add humor, when appropriate, to get attention and make your message memorable. You'll undoubtedly recall political cartoons you've seen in newspapers and magazines; humor can be just as effective as a sledgehammer in getting your message across.

COURSE EVALUATIONS

Good Model

Subject: DFU's Revenue Accounting in the Oil and Gas Industry--
            Seminar Critique

Having been in the oil-and-gas industry for two years, I was already familiar with much of what the April 23-24 DFU's Revenue Accounting seminar covered. I did profit, however, from the instructor's discussions of the Windfall Profits Tax and NGPA.

In the future, I recommend that we send only those who have had less than one year's experience in the industry. If we have as many as six persons who need this basic training, I'd suggest contacting DFU directly (373-467-1234) to arrange the course in-house for a cost of approximately $2,700 versus outside attendance at $425 per participant.

The presentation involved thought-provoking analysis of specific job assignments and well-organized lectures covering the basic revenue accounting functions both in gas and oil. The instructor, Wayne Hew, provided class sets of various government publications so that we could follow along directly as he made application. Mr. Hew seems very knowledgeable in the revenue accounting field with 18 years' experience at Ryan Corporation and three years with the DFU Continuing Education Department. Articulate and receptive to questions from the group, he made specific on-the-job applications yet never let the discussions ramble.

For an extensive list of his course topics, see the attached brochure.

Do's _____

• Use the basic functional format. The message of interest, of course, is not the course's content or simply your attendance, but rather what you thought of the course. Was it beneficial to you? Why? Or why not? Be specific, avoiding such broad strokes as, "It will enhance my job performance."

• Evaluate the course objectively. In addition to commenting on personal benefit, critique the course as it might benefit others: Did the course meet stated objectives? Was the material slanted to the appropriate audience? How knowledgeable, prepared, articulate, or organized was the instructor? What methods did the instructor employ—lecture, role play, films? Were there adequate opportunities for class questions? Did discussions center around theory or application? Were there handouts, books, complimentary member-ships that will be of future benefit?

• Be specific about content. List some key topics and/or attach a course outline if possible.

• Make a judgment about sending others if you were a first-time attendee from your department or company. In other words, "interpret" your critique. If the course was beneficial, was it beneficial enough for your supervisor to send others? Should the training be mandatory for all employees handling related responsibilities? Or do you consider the training relatively insignificant for your particular job assignment?

• If you are recommending that others attend an off-site course or that you schedule the course in-house, include a cost analysis. Also, give all necessary information to follow up your recommendation—contact person, address, phone number.

• Mention the instructor's credentials. These details either add to or detract from the value of the course. In some cases, an instructor's credentials may be the basis of deciding between Course A and Course B.

DIRECTIVES

Weak Models

Subject: Copy Machine Use

The largest collating copier located on the second floor has been installed for use by Materials and Services personnel only. It's the responsibility of everyone in the building to show common courtesy in scheduling large copying tasks so as not to prohibit day-to-day operations in all sections.

◆ ◆ ◆

Subject: Protocol for Phone Calls

Once more I must remind you that there are some members in the field who violate protocol and make phone calls to various staff members in Boston, asking for particular business and personal favors. This must stop once and for all!

In the past I have requested from you an explanation of each week's long-distance calls to both Boston and Los Angeles. Some of you have complied; some have ignored the directive. Only emergency calls should be made to Boston and Los Angeles; all other favors or requests should come through my office.

I will be monitoring this situation carefully in the future.

Don'ts

- Don't bury your directive in implications. In the first example, what exactly is the directive? That no one in the building other than Materials and Services personnel may use the second-floor copier for any reason—emergency or otherwise? That Materials and Services people should not tie up the copier for long periods of time? That people in other departments should be more courteous in scheduling large tasks so as not to force others to go to the second-floor machine? That large tasks should be done before or after peak hours? Remember that even though your intention may be to soften the directive, your reader may not infer what you intend.
- Don't be arbitrary. When possible, give reasons for the directive. Why is the phone-call protocol necessary?
- Don't fail to give all details necessary to take the action, or inaction, as the case may be. For instance, how should readers of the second memo distinguish between emergency and "regular" calls? What are the guidelines?

● Don't use "fight" words such as "ignored," "failed to," "refused," even "must" at times. Such words emphasize a negative and hostile attitude.
● Don't resort to sarcasm.

Good Models

Subject: Air-Conditioning Filter Screens

Since our discussion three weeks ago, nothing has been done to correct the problem about the air-conditioning filter screens. Please install them immediately and confirm to me in writing when they are in place.

Apparently you disagree with my opinion that the cost of the manpower involved in testing for the exact problem is prohibitive. Nevertheless, whether the screens do or do not solve our problem, this ounce of prevention should be our first step.

If you have any problems in the installation process, please let me know so that we can work them out immediately.

◆ ◆ ◆

Subject: Audiometric Examinations

You have been scheduled for an audiometric exam at the Clareton Office on May 5 at 8:00 a.m. Please complete the attached Hearing Conservation Record before reporting for the exam. Answer all questions to the best of your ability, and have your employee identification number and Social Security number ready for the examiner.

The test is required as a "base line" audiogram with which subsequent audiograms will be compared to measure any hearing loss.

For us to have the most accurate test possible, your cooperation is essential. Please observe the following:
1. You should be free of workplace noise for at least fourteen hours prior to the exam. If this is impossible, use disposable earplugs while working.
2. Avoid exposure to loud noise (loud music, gunfire, motorcycles, auto races, etc.) during off-duty time for at least fourteen hours prior to the exam.

If you have any questions about the exam or your preparation, contact me at extension 5729.

Do's

- State the clear, firm directive upfront. If necessary, ask the subordinate to verify compliance.
- Give reasons for your directives when you can. Giving reasons does not suggest weakness or the need for justification of your decisions. Instead, reasons help the reader to determine whether to approach you again if the situation or circumstances change, thus allowing correction. People cooperate better with a "why" even when they don't agree.
- Give all details and guidelines to accomplish the directive. Include times, dates, costs, preparation, procedures, and follow-up expected. Missing details provide an escape hatch for reluctant followers.
- Acknowledge that the reader may not agree with your evaluation of the situation, but be firm about your directive nonetheless.
- Include courtesy words even when you have authority to command.

DISMISSALS

Good Models

Subject: Dismissal--Bill Wright

This memo is to document termination of Bill Wright as lab technician, effective March 10, 198-. Bill has demonstrated that he cannot be dependable in his performance or attendance.

The following incidents have been discussed with Bill on five occasions (each noted in his personnel file) but with no improvement:

	Performance Record
October 16, 198-	Failure to be in the lab during regular work hours
November 11, 198-	Failure to be in the lab during regular work hours
December 21, 198-	Violation of safety rules--smoking
January 31, 198-	Negligence of assigned responsibility
February 24, 198-	Violation of safety rules--smoking

	Attendance Record
Fourth Quarter, 198-	Five absences and two tardies
First Quarter, 198-	Eight absences and four tardies

Bill's undependability has made it necessary to pay other personnel overtime to make up for his absence or lack of performance and has inhibited smooth operation of research techniques.

◆ ◆ ◆

Subject: [Leave subject line blank.]

Shirley,

As you know, sales have declined steadily over the past eighteen months; as of June 30, 198-, we have recorded our lowest earnings in the past eight years. The sluggish economy and increased competition for our market share have forced us to restructure our work force and eliminate several positions from the middle-management rung. I regret to say that yours has been one of those positions eliminated. Effective Friday, May 15, 198-, you will be laid off with those benefits for which you are now eligible.

During the next three weeks, please feel free to make your primary effort that of locating a new position within Howell-Forrester--if that's possible in these times--or outside the company. Also, we encourage you to phone Employee Relations Manager Frank Hanover for an appointment to discuss your search for employment.

Attached is an outline of your benefits and conversion options with regard to pension and insurance plans. If there are any questions about these, contact Michael Smith at extension 3377.

I sincerely regret that business conditions require this action, and I offer you my personal help in your efforts to find another position that affords you a much-deserved opportunity to further your career.

◆   ◆   ◆

Subject: Dismissal Investigation

As Martha Greenwall promised you on the phone April 12, we have reviewed the facts with regard to your dismissal from Krantz Industries.

Each of the statements you made in your April 10 memo has been thoroughly investigated; in fact, we have interviewed employees on three levels of the organization to discover and substantiate all facts and evaluations surrounding the situation. After our careful investigation and documentation of the issues, we have decided that your termination is the best solution for all concerned.

Let me assure you, however, that our policy on giving reference is to release only the dates of your employment, job title, and salary schedule. And, of course, requests for salary information must be in writing.

We do wish you every success in your future employment.

Do's _____

• Use the basic functional format when the memo is only file documentation of dismissal. If, however, you are writing directly to the employee to be dismissed, follow these special guidelines for presenting "bad news": Begin on a neutral note, give reasons for the termination, and then word the dismissal as positively as possible. If the dismissal is not due to an employee's poor work record, you don't want to splash cold water in his or her face before providing a towel.

• Be truthful, objective, and clear in stating any reasons for dismissal. False or ambiguous statements, even if meant to protect the employee's ego, may be used against you if your decision is later challenged. Although you may not wish to state all details and reasons in a memo addressed to the employee, make sure documented reasons appear in file memos.

- Show concern. In the case of a layoff, remind the employee of benefits he or she has—finances, outplacement services, or positive referrals and contacts. If it is your or the company's policy to avoid giving bad references, assure an employee who has been dismissed for poor performance that he or she will not be "blacklisted."
- Use a matter-of-fact, not vindictive, tone.

ERRORS, TO POINT OUT ANOTHER'S

Weak Models

Subject: Expense Account Receipts

Deductible expenses for company travel must be supported by actual receipts--not photocopies of the receipts. We have noted that several receipts attached to your expense account dated August 15, 198- are copies rather than originals.

Although we are processing your expense account for payment this time, photocopies of receipts will not be acceptable in the future.

◆   ◆   ◆

Subject: Handling Incentive Payments

One more time, everybody. Although some of you have been handling incentive computations for years, I still find persistent errors. For the last time, I do hope we can get this straight!

You are to send <u>three</u> (not one, not two) copies of the incentive computation forms. After I review and approve the forms, <u>I</u> will send one to the sales rep and one to Beaumont, and then keep one for my files. Each of you has a copy machine; please use it.

When you do your computations on the sales split, be sure to compute your figures accurately--I have found several errors here again.

Please, if you have further questions about this record-keeping system, call me before you send the forms. I would appreciate your assistance in doing this correctly.

Don'ts

● Don't patronize. Even the insertion of courtesy words such as "please" and "appreciate" fails to compensate for sarcasm. Watch unusual punctuation marks and underlined words to avoid "screaming" in print. Also, avoid showing your "tolerance" in overlooking or correcting another's error.

● Don't assume the error is intentional or due to carelessness. Consider the possibility that your instructions have been unclear or that circumstances prevented compliance or perfection. At the very least, consider that the reader may not have been aware of the importance of accuracy. Assume some of the responsibility for the error yourself.

● Don't focus on the error to the exclusion of how the matter should be corrected. Your memo should not begin a game of "Gotcha."

● Don't exaggerate results of the error. If the reader thinks you have overplayed the subject, he'll compensate by playing down its importance.

Good Models

Subject: Handling Incentive Payments

There are still some problems in routing incentive forms and computing payments. Let me repeat the procedure for handling such forms:

> Send three copies of the incentive-computation forms to me. After I review and approve the forms, I'll send one to the sales rep and one to Beaumont and then keep one for my files.

Please make a special effort to recheck all computations before they leave your office. We do not have the manpower to do this double-checking here. When checks go out incorrectly and must be returned and reprocessed, the cost goes up considerably, not to mention the inconvenience of the delayed payment.

If you have any questions at all about this record-keeping system and routing or about computing unusual splits, please call me before sending the forms. I appreciate your help in handling these correctly.

◆   ◆   ◆

Subject: Cash-Forecast Formats

Enclosed you will find the assumptions used for the February–April 198- cash forecast; we'd appreciate having your next cash forecast sent in this format. In fact, you may want to copy this form to use in developing all your information.

If you have any suggestions for still further improvements, please let us know.

◆   ◆   ◆

Subject: Leasehold Improvements--Account 468

Thanks for your memo on the Cedarpoint account (#468); I do understand your reasoning behind expending the costs for remodeling the headquarters office.

In my opinion, however, these expenditures should be accounted for as leasehold improvements. Here's my reasoning:
1. The improvement's useful life exceeds one year.
2. Generally accepted practice is to capitalize and depreciate these improvements over the remaining term of the lease.

I'd like to give this further thought and talk to Ed Weese before I ask you to make definite changes. If I'm wrong, let me assure you, it won't be the first time.

Do's

● Begin on a neutral note. Then "creep up" on the error if you can. Notice that in the cash-forecast memo, the writer simply offers a better method to accomplish the task rather than pointing out the deficiency per se. Passive-voice constructions can be useful here: "In the future, spare parts should be sent by air freight." (You do not say that the sender has made a mistake this time.) At other times, you can walk around a direct assault with a "there are problems" approach, as in the revised incentive-payment model.

● Focus on what you have done or what the reader should do to correct the problem rather than trying to assign blame.

● Emphasize the importance of accuracy.

● Suggest precautions against future problems.

● Show diffidence and humility.

For further guidelines in addressing errors, see "Complaints," page 53 and following.

ERRORS, TO ADMIT YOUR OWN

Weak Model

Subject: Boyton Contracts

I deeply regret my error in mailing the Boyton contracts to Mr.
Jorgensen's old address. It's our policy always to verify new and existing
addresses by phone before we mail any such documents. I don't know how
we could possibly have overlooked this client's address.

Certainly, I can understand why Mr. Jorgensen was so upset when he
phoned you yesterday about the delay. If he had called here, I would have
been glad to assure him that the error was completely mine. Please let me
assure you that this kind of error does not happen often, because I realize
the importance of a timely signature.

The returned contracts went out today by Express Mail; I do hope this
mistake has not jeopardized the negotiations in any way. My sincerest
apologies; this won't happen again.

Don'ts

- Don't "bleed" all over the memo. Briefly explain how the error happened and then focus on the correction.
- Don't be dramatic. Remember that all errors are not created equal. Overblown apologies and explanations sound insincere.
- Don't promise that the error will never occur again. Rather, state what actions you have taken to correct the problem this time and to make its reoccurrence less likely.

Good Models

Subject: Incorrect Number on Pumping Order

Yes, my scheduler did indeed make an error on the attached pumping
order; he used the custody index number rather than the transfer code.

I have cautioned him about confusing the numbers on future orders and
have asked him to check his hard copy of all orders after they have been
entered into the computer.

Since we've had trouble before, I should have given closer supervision here. Please let me know if you uncover still other such errors; I'll follow them up immediately.

♦ ♦ ♦

Subject: Patton Island Sketches

In reviewing the Patton Island sketches forwarded to your office yesterday, I notice that I've made a miscalculation on the sleeve length regarding attachment of the clip angles. The correct length should be 28″ rather than 29″. The shorter length will allow the angles to sit nearly flush against the left side.

Everything else about the sketches seems to be in good order. But I did want to get this information to you immediately, even though I know you don't plan to review the plans for another few weeks.

Do's

- State the error *and* correction immediately.
- Evaluate the seriousness of your mistake; explain and apologize accordingly.
- When the situation has political undertones to your disadvantage, play down the error with a matter-of-fact tone. After all, everybody makes mistakes. On the other hand, a poor-me approach can work sometimes—that is, exaggerate the seriousness of the error and be profuse in your apology so that your reader must console you that things "aren't that bad." However, "bleed" only when you know the politics involved and the likely reaction of your reader to your play for sympathy.
- Take responsibility for errors that come from your office; don't pass the buck to subordinates even though they may have made the error. After all, you are the supervisor.
- Report and correct the error immediately. Delay usually compounds the problem.

EXPENSES, TO CUT, WATCH, OR JUSTIFY

Weak Model

Subject: Mailing and Printing Costs

I have just come from the supply room; boxes and boxes of <u>Bylines</u> and thousands and thousands of financial statements are stacked around the room. Why? Obviously, you are printing too many copies of each, and that, in turn, creates a huge mailing cost in shipping excessive copies to all the branches.

Wayne, this is a function of your department. What have you done to develop a savings in mailing? What kind of controls do you have for not ordering hundreds of thousands of dollars of extra printing? Something has to be done immediately.

As I review the operations of various offices across the country, I find over and over that those managers who control the checkbook and watch expenses make profits. Rarely do the big spenders pay attention to reviewing costs and rarely do they make a profit in difficult times.

I'm sending a copy of this memo to all I think are involved in this plethora of printing and mailing, hoping you can get together with them to work out something to alleviate this problem.

Don'ts

- Don't base your request to cut or watch expenses on personal observation alone. You need facts to back up what you say; otherwise, the reader will likely argue that you have latched onto the "exceptional." If you don't want to gather the facts yourself, then ask the responsible person (perhaps your reader) to do so. Without authoritative data, the issue remains vague.
- Don't sound abrasive. In a "problem" statement, calling someone by name in direct address ("Wayne, this is a function of your department."), you have made the issue a personal attack. Including yourself in a we-need-to-cut-or-watch-expenses statement makes a much more palatable suggestion. Also, watch implications. The above model implies that Wayne is one of the "big spenders" who rarely makes a profit.
- Don't reprimand by way of a cutting-expenses memo sent to more than one reader. In pointing out someone's weakness, communicate individually, not with a distribution list.

Good Models

Subject: Reducing Mailing and Printing Costs

Wayne, what can we do to reduce our mailing and printing costs? Down in the supply room, I noticed boxes and boxes of <u>Bylines</u> and last month's financial statements; I assume these were leftover copies.

I'd like you to do some kind of study of our actual printing and mailing costs and then see what we might do to control these expenditures. Here are some suggestions for your consideration:
* Manual audit of mailouts from each branch
* Duplications from corporate and branches
* Combining financial statements and <u>Bylines</u> into one publication
* Cheaper mailing rates
* Survey of distribution problems

We need to control the checkbook and watch pennies to make profits in these difficult times. Your suggestions for printing and mailing controls will ensure that we do that. Thanks for your help; I'll look forward to your conclusions.

◆ ◆ ◆

Subject: Justification for an Additional Tape Librarian

Unless we hire another librarian immediately, the library will become nonfunctional. The burden on one individual to monitor, maintain, and perform tape-librarian functions has exceeded our expectations. Although temporary help has been used from time to time, errors are on the increase due to lack of training and rushed work of all concerned.

The ROT-WPF library currently houses 22,000 tapes, and that number increases daily. The tape-evaluator operator may assist the librarian from time to time, but this extra responsibility detracts from our evaluation process. Temporary help leaves us vulnerable to numerous costly mistakes; one week's audit revealed that we had approximately 16 such errors involving 22 lost hours to locate and correct the mistakes.

Why did we not budget for this manpower need? First, we did not expect the rapid business growth or the expansion on the TN420. Our database has increased 43 percent in the past year. Second, we anticipated the removal of our RW500; but, as the situation now stands, we plan either to convert or merge this database into the TN420.

I propose that this new librarian work a delayed first shift to allow maximum overlapping coverage for six hours of the eight-hour shift.

Clearly, this approximate $900 labor cost per month is insignificant compared to revenue losses due to errors or delays.

Do's

• Use the basic functional format, stating the expense of concern immediately. Even in a persuasive memo, your reader still needs to know to what conclusion you intend to lead him. Without knowing the "bottom line" message, he feels manipulated. Another inherent danger in building your case before making your request is that your reader may examine your evidence and arrive at an altogether different conclusion. By giving your statement of "wants" first, you can guide his thinking toward your own conclusion.

• Include a *why*. Readers need motivation for both belt-tightening and spending.

• Translate vague costs to specific, understandable dollars. Personal observation alone carries limited weight. Note that the writer of the second memo has kept a log of one week's errors and translated them into hours lost. Could you survey others for their opinions? Talk to experts from inside and outside the company? Do a literature search? Keep a log of the situation? Identify exact causes and calculate real savings or expenses?

• When ordering a "cut," offer alternatives. Suggest ways to accomplish the same activities with fewer dollars. Pinpoint your priorities for spending.

• When justifying expenses, anticipate alternative solutions and address them. What limitations do these other options have? You'll notice that in the last model the writer mentions difficulties in using temporary help or assigning the tape evaluator these extra librarian duties.

• Assume your part in the situation, making your reader feel that thrift is a team effort.

• Describe the financial climate accurately. You don't want to sound so ominous that you create panic among the employees and have them scrambling for jobs elsewhere. Neither do you want to start a game of "Wolf, Wolf."

EXPENSES, REIMBURSEMENTS

Good Models

Subject: Request for Invoice Under DBC Contract #2005

On March 15, 198-, Bloomington Service Company of Shreveport, Louisiana, loaded 17,779.5 net barrels of natural gasoline onboard the <u>Barrymore 2300</u> under tow of the <u>Esther R.</u> This was the third delivery on contract #2005; the contract has a remaining balance of 8,000 barrels to be delivered. Freight for this shipment totals $5,800.

Please invoice DBC for this product and associated freight. Since our next delivery to DBC is scheduled for March 28, we recommend special handling and courier delivery of this invoice.

If you have questions about payment, please phone me at 7878.

◆ ◆ ◆

Subject: Stolen Expense Check

My expense reimbursement check ($1,048.88) for the period of March 4, 198- to March 9, 198- has been stolen. I have notified our Treasurer to stop payment; now I need a replacement check.

Attached for your convenience is a copy of the original expense report, along with copies of the original receipts.

◆ ◆ ◆

Subject: Reimbursement for Home Closing

The enclosed reimbursement check for $5,428.32 covers the following closing costs of your new home at 12345 Hamilton Drive, Beachport, CA:
* 1 percent loan origination fee
* 2 percent discount points
* legal fees
* title policy

If you need a further breakdown of these costs, please contact Charles Ivy at extension 4580.

Do's

• State upfront the exact expense, product, or service for which you are reimbursing or requesting reimbursement.

• Include all identifying details such as costs, contract or invoice numbers, dates, delivery methods, installment plans, addresses, receipts, explanations, special handling requirements, and deadlines. In other words, anticipate confusion or error; then eliminate it.

FAREWELLS

Good Models

Subject: Retirement of Anna Fitzgerald

Effective February 1, 198-, Anna Fitzgerald will no longer have to trudge through wind and snow to arrive at a paper-covered desk and ringing telephone by 8:30 every morning; she is retiring.

I can't think of anyone in the department who has done more to lift spirits with her "witticisms for every occasion" than Anna. Certainly, she's the only one who holds all departmental secrets, such as where to find spare file-cabinet keys, a copy of an annual report from 1945, or the name and phone number of the maintenance manager in Kalamazoo. Let's hope she doesn't get an unlisted number and remains available in our inevitable times of crisis.

Join me in congratulating Anna on her richly deserved independence and leisure. We'll miss you, Anna, but we wish you the best with future plans to travel and show your paintings.

Subject: Resignation of Max Nicholas

It's with regret that I announce the resignation of Max Nicholas as Sales Manager, effective September 30, 198-. Since Max joined our staff in 1978, he has hired, trained, and motivated many of you to become top performers in your field. I'm sure you regret his leaving as much as we at headquarters do.

It is with warmest personal regards that we wish Max success as he assumes his new position, Director of Sales for the International Division at Meridian Corporation.

Do's

- Be sincere; avoid flowery, overblown sentiment.
- Be informal.
- Be personal without being too familiar. Comment on pleasant personality traits, contributions to the company, or future plans. Remember, however, that retirement or resignation may not be a pleasant experience for everyone; avoid remarks about age, conflict, illness, finances.

FOLLOW-UPS

Weak Model

Subject: Light-Pipe Paper Information

Hong, I sent the rough draft of my light-pipe paper to you on May 13, more than six months ago. I also asked that you provide further data of relative flux versus length for a 3mm-diameter light pipe. I have received nothing from you yet. I realize that you were out of town for several weeks, but this work would take perhaps one day at most.

At this point, I ask that you send the data to complete the paper in the next three weeks, or I shall proceed without it. I really don't think this is an unreasonable request.

Don'ts

- Don't imply that the reader is negligent or incompetent.
- Don't sound self-righteous.
- Don't use a whining or threatening tone.
- Don't take away all the reader's excuses. In the above memo, how can the reader defend himself, should he want to comply with the request? The writer has backed him into a corner and made any reply an embarrassment. Leave your reader room to excuse his delay or failure; your only concern should be that he follow through with the project.

Good Models

Subject: Production Staffing in New York

As we discussed in the staff meeting on October 2, we have three unfilled positions in our Production Department in New York, all three of which are critical to proceeding with the Sinclair project. The personnel budget will need to be increased by $88,000, as I have outlined it.

Could you please give me a call to let me know the status of the manpower request submitted September 26?

◆ ◆ ◆

Subject: Flyers for the Sales Convention

All information for the flyers to be distributed at the Arapahoe Convention next month is complete and ready for typesetting except the figures for special discounts for bulk film orders.

Have you had time to set up the special discount rates I mentioned in my June 5 memo?

The layout will have to go to the typesetter by Friday, June 18, at the latest. I do hope we can include your information before that date, because the flyer will be much more effective in drawing calls with that special discount rate in black and white before prospective clients.

Do's

- Restate your original message and request for action.
- Identify the first communication by subject rather than by date alone. If an original memo or phone message was lost, misplaced, or misrouted, the reader may not know what you're talking about.
- If appropriate, use the if-I-don't-hear-from-you-by approach; state your next action if no response is forthcoming. In the last memo, the writer implies the brochure will go to the printer on June 18—with or without the requested information.
- Offer an excuse for your reader's failure to reply—one that will allow him to save face for having failed to respond by the specified date or to acknowledge receipt of your request or message. Even a phrase such as, "Could you let me know the status of . . ." implies some progress.
- Repeat all details—about who, what, when, where, why, how, how much—that were included the first time around. Don't rely on past correspondence that may not have been received.
- Emphasize the critical need for a response. If you can, find reader incentive for the action.
- Enclose a copy of the original memo only when the subject is too long or complicated to be repeated easily in the present reminder. Otherwise, doing so seems to be "proofing yourself" or documenting the reader's failure to reply or comply.

HIRING

Good Model

Subject: Joan Davidson--Applicant for Technical Writing Instructor/
             Consultant

With a varied background in both writing and speaking, Joan Davidson
demonstrates the ability to design and deliver curriculum material in an
articulate manner. Although she lacks experience in sales, Joan seems
eager to participate in our training program to overcome this void. I
recommend we hire her as Technical Writing Instructor/Consultant at a
starting salary of $28,000.

Strengths

* B.A., M.A. in journalism
* Extensive writing experience: has published papers in major
  social-sciences and engineering journals; has published college-level
  text supplement for writing course; has written and edited training
  manuals, employee handbooks, procedures for several major
  corporations; has written advertising copy for local and national
  bookstore chains; has published three plays.
* Good verbal skills: has presented papers at three national
  conferences; has taught business writing and technical writing
  courses at two junior colleges for a total of six years; is permanent
  fill-in for local TV talk-show host; was articulate during interview
  and fielded questions about handling client situations well.
* Pleasant personality: is open to suggestions about training; shows
  evidence of creative problem-solving skills; is self-motivated.

Weakness

* No formal sales experience: suggest training program and
  self-directed study, to which applicant wholeheartedly has agreed.

I have made a thorough check of all references; former employers have
nothing but praise for her teaching skills, her writing efforts, and her
on-the-job consulting and client relationships arranged through their
offices. They verify that her reasons for leaving past jobs have to do solely
with lack of opportunity for advancement.

After reviewing approximately 60 resumes and conducting 15 interviews,
I'm convinced that Joan is the best-qualified candidate for this position and
will make a valuable, long-term contribution to Harper. Her complete
resume is attached.

Do's

- Give a brief summary judgment about the applicant's strengths and weaknesses. Follow with your recommendation for bypassing or hiring the applicant at what position and for what salary.
- Interpret facts as they appear on a resume and make judgments. Highlight and comment on experience and skills only as they apply to the needs of your company's position. For example, in the preceding memo, writing, verbal, and sales skills are the chief criteria for the job. The writing experience, therefore, has been lifted nearly verbatim from the applicant's resume. The verbal skills, however, have been pulled together from varied experience and are highlighted in an altogether different arrangement from the chronological listing on the original resume.
- Summarize information gained from references.
- Let the approver know how extensive your search has been.
- Use lists and brief phrases just as you would in a resume to allow your reader to skim highlights quickly.
- Attach a copy of the applicant's resume (if one has been prepared) in case the approver wants to verify your interpretations and conclusions.

INFORMATION, REQUESTS FOR

Good Models

Subject: Charge-offs--Information on the Responsible Person

So that we might route our correspondence with regard to charge-offs to the correct individual at your branch, we would like you to fill out the attached sheet and return it to our office by March 31, 198-.

It has been our understanding that the charge-off coordinator handled all aspects of charge-off accounts. In our dealings with the various branches over the past six months, however, we have discovered that some of the duties pertaining to charge-offs have been delegated to other personnel. Your supplying the names of the individuals who handle this duty will help both your office and ours receive correspondence and direct phone inquiries more quickly.

◆ ◆ ◆

Subject: Budget Preparation for 198-
            Requested Information and Timetables

Spring is the time of year for baseball, true love, and budget preparations. Yes, budget preparations. And to avoid the last-minute crunch, we are beginning immediately.

The budgeting section will be forwarding a newly revised form accompanied by complete instructions for you to develop departmental data. Please observe the following timetable in preparing and submitting your information:

	Review in District Office	Review in General Office	Ready for Authorized Approval
Personnel	5/17	5/28	6/14
Vehicle	6/7	6/21	7/12
Operations	7/26	8/2	8/20
Capital Projects	8/6	8/13	9/1

These dates are designed to give each of you ample time to evaluate needs and still allow us time to consolidate the overall budget in our office.

Now, let's get to the specifics: Please provide a concise justification for all requested items and staff. Capital budget items requiring engineering estimates should be submitted to R. W. Bimble by May 1. T. C. Willis,

Director of Training, will provide to all managers by May 1 information on tuition and related expenses for all schools, seminars, and conventions.

With good organization and planning, we can meet the deadlines for final budget approval with accurate, complete information--maybe even in time to watch a few baseball games.

Do's

- Focus immediately on the information you need. Don't make your request a by-the-way item toward the end of the memo.
- Be specific in all questions you want answered and, if important, state the format in which you want the information provided.
- Tell why you need the information if the reason is not obvious. Occasionally, when readers don't understand the necessity for some action or information, they "pick and choose" what data they think you need rather than respond with what you want.
- Emphasize due dates. Phrases such as "at your earliest convenience" may be intended as a courtesy, but they invite procrastination; if you have a due date in mind, say so. Be careful to avoid the double-due-date effect— that is, if you are requesting information that you in turn will incorporate into your own work and then supply to someone else, don't state both dates. Such an explanation lets the reader know the "grace" period built in for yourself. The two dates, therefore, become leeway (in the reader's mind) for getting the information to you. For special emphasis put the due date in a paragraph by itself.
- Make the action easy to take. When you can, provide forms or examples to ensure that you get all necessary data in an acceptable format.
- Anticipate the reader's steps in preparing the information. The more questions you can answer before they're asked, the sooner you'll get your information. In the last memo, the writer anticipated the need for engineering estimates and training costs.
- Provide incentive for the reader to cooperate. In the first memo, that means a simple statement about properly directed correspondence and phone inquiries. In the second memo, however, the writer has tried a touch of humor in his mention of free time for baseball rather than overtime for budgeting. Remember the usual mound of paper your memo must compete with for attention; make your requests stand out.

INSPECTIONS

Weak Model

Subject: Off-Site Storage Audit

We presently occupy space in a data-storage building on Brice and Hitton streets. This space is a bin area constructed of metal shelves with solid metal backs, bolted together to form a room (approximately 9′ × 16′ × 10′) with a cement floor, iron-grating ceiling, and wire door for access. This door is locked by supervisory building personnel during normal shift hours, 8:00 a.m. to 5:00 p.m.

This area is cooled from a single-unit, rooftop A/C unit with no redundant capacity. Presently this storage bin area is shared with other tenants. The building is located three miles from our data center and within safe limits from hazards. There do not seem to be adequate controls for computer-room environmental control; dust migration is also a problem. Access is available to this area at all times of the day and night. Two sprinkler heads in our area make fire protection adequate. Environmental control also is lacking at times when deliverymen leave overhead doors open for long periods of time.

I recommend that we terminate use of this present storage bin and secure space in a different area of the building, an area that provides single-tenant control. We cannot allow access to our area by others. However, history suggests that existing environmental control is adequate. As stated before, fire protection is good and access to the area by the fire department is acceptable. It should be noted that if total security of our tapes is to be provided, the only solution would be a fire/heatproof safe. Security of the present site is okay, but we lack complete control. All doors of egress are alarmed, and there is adequate personnel to supervise tenant activities. But one thing I noticed was that with multitenant space bins, it is possible for one tenant to remove another tenant's material without the knowledge of building personnel. This situation should be corrected.

We are currently paying $150 rent per year. The cost for moving into the recommended space, which will provide improved environmental control and improved security, will be $170 per month, an increased cost of $1,890 per year.

Don'ts _____

● Don't organize your memo by chronological order of inspection.
● Don't begin with background information that the reader either already knows or doesn't care to know.

- Don't vacillate between the "adequate" and the "inadequate." This confusing mixture of details makes it difficult for the reader to keep score on how the situation really stands without marking a tally sheet as he reads.
- Don't make judgmental statements without identifying them as such. Separate fact from opinion, and acknowledge where others may disagree.
- Don't put a lengthy list of recommendations in a separate section from findings and force the reader to go back and forth from page to page (finding to recommendation, back to finding, back to recommendation) to understand and do the recommended action. A separate "Findings" section is appropriate only in the following cases: when the findings are lengthy, complicated, and in need of detailed explanation.

Good Models

Subject: Off-Site Storage Audit

Our present data-storage bin in the building on Brice and Hitton streets is inadequate for environmental control and security reasons. I recommend that we terminate use of our present bin and secure space in the same building but in an area that provides single-tenant control of access. The increased cost of this recommended space with improved environmental control and security will be $1,890 per year.

Our present storage space is a bin constructed of metal shelves with solid metal backs, bolted together to form a room (approximately 9' × 16' × 10') with a cement floor, iron-grating ceiling, and wire door for access. This door is locked by supervisory building personnel during normal shift hours, 8:00 a.m. to 5:00 p.m. However, we have access to this area at all times of the day and night. Other tenants have access to our area during the normal shift times; it is possible for one tenant to remove another tenant's material without the knowledge of building personnel.

The building, located three miles from our data center, lies within safe limits from hazards. Two sprinkler heads in our area allow access by the fire department. Dust migration, however, and other temperature controls are lacking when deliverymen leave overhead doors open for long periods of time. Although total security for our tapes would require a fire/heatproof safe, I do not think the expense is justified at this time.

Currently we are paying $150 rent per year. The charge for the recommended single-tenant space will be $170 per month, for an overall increase of $1,890.

◆ ◆ ◆

Subject: Audit of Lackland Operations

Our on-site audit team found the operation at Lackland to be efficient with only two exceptions: lack of informational signs and fire safety.

We submit the following recommendations for your consideration and ask that you review and comment on them by April 10, 198-.

Recommendations for Signs
* Signs at all four entrances to the site (information to be included: plant name, address, emergency phone numbers, "no smoking" warning)
* Sign on Williamsburg Road cutoff (information to be included: plant name, address, directional arrow)

Recommendations for Fire Safety
* Study on adequacy of firewalls around the storage tanks
* Hydrotesting of fire extinguishers at five-year intervals
* Written procedures for fire drills and emergency evacuations. (Sample procedures from the Oakland plant are attached as guidelines.)

This inspection team included A. B. Wall, P. T. Bailey, and T. H. Williams. Please direct questions to any one of them at extension 6667.

◆　◆　◆

Subject: Residential Inspection at 2500 Morris

At your request, I inspected the house at 2500 Morris on January 8, 198-. Based on my limited visual inspection, I think the house needs immediate foundational and roofing repair before we can attempt to market it.

The foundation has experienced differential movement to a more than normal degree. The roof is nonserviceable on the north half of the garage. The basic structural framing, including load-bearing walls and vertical bracing, appears to be functional as intended with one exception: The front porch is in poor condition due to wood rot.

Deterioration of nonstructural materials requires repair, but not immediately.

Flashing caps loose. Have Lenny Holloway make these repairs before the heavy rains cause further drainage problems.

Attic insulation missing. Recommend that we add after the house is sold.

Exterior paint cracked. Schedule painting job with Kemkoe Painters, Inc., at their earliest convenience. The house will not sell without new paint job. I would suggest we keep the original color if at all possible to match it.

Do's

● State your overall evaluation results briefly upfront—"serious problems with . . . ," "minor problems only," "adequate," "inadequate and in need of immediate attention," "adequate with the exception of . . ." Then make each area of inspection into a "mini" basic functional format. Choose the most logical arrangement to present specific findings—by department, by most to least significant, by most to least expensive, by physical layout, or any other easy-to-follow arrangement. Under each finding, insert your recommended action to correct or improve the item, area, or procedure. Then follow with specific details—usually how and why. Why did the problem or deficiency develop? How should we do the action and/or how should we prevent future problems? Last, under each separate section, mention any attachment you have included to make the action clearer.

● In lengthy inspections, make sure headings are frequent and informative to allow multiple readers to skim and single out their area of interest and action.

● When your memo is a lateral communication, use a deferential tone. Notice the second paragraph in the "Audit of Lackland Operations" memo.

INTRODUCTIONS
(of employees, products, equipment, services, forms)

Good Models

Subject: New Employee--Bill Fritz

Effective September 10, Bill Fritz will join our department as a computer programmer, reporting to Tom Symonds.

Bill has formerly worked with Sewell-Spencer Corporation, where he served as an associate programmer. In that position, he gained valuable experience in both maintenance and development programming, as well as in operations support. Bill is a graduate of Ohio University with a specialization in management information systems. On leisurely weekends, you'll find Bill enjoying his favorite hobbies--trout fishing or racquetball.

Since Bill is from out of state, join me in welcoming him to our staff, our state, and our Southern life-style. Welcome aboard, Bill.

◆　◆　◆

Subject: New Reference Booklet on Tube Feedings

A new reference booklet entitled <u>Tube-Feeding Formulas</u> is now available to all dietitians, dietetic interns, and nurses. The information is designed as a reference for ordering proper tube feedings for patients unable to eat. Key topics include the ordering of calories, protein, carbohydrates, fats, sodium, and potassium.

Formulating diets for each patient through the tedious task of searching scattered reference sources will no longer be necessary. With this new booklet as an authoritative and standard source, patients should more readily accept diets prescribed for them.

You'll note that the booklet is designed in the 7×4 size to fit easily into our <u>Nurses' Handbook.</u> Both, of course, will still be sold separately. The price of the booklet is $1.49. To our knowledge, this information is not available in this compact format at this low price from any other company.

If your customers would like to examine the booklet to determine its usefulness to particular groups before ordering in quantity, we'd be happy to furnish them with a free copy. Simply phone Marilyn Graham at extension 222 and give her the customer's mailing address. She will be glad to handle this mailing detail for you and to refer the customer to the appropriate representative for follow-up.

Even though your customers will not be our primary market, we have enclosed a copy of the booklet so that you will be able to field any questions about it.

◆ ◆ ◆

Subject: New Dictating Equipment

The Milton transcriber equipment for the Word Processing Center is now available. We're excited about the increased productivity this new equipment will allow, and we encourage each of you to take advantage of this simple writing method.

I've arranged for a Milton consultant to conduct 20 user sessions during the week of April 12–16. Sessions will begin at 8:00, 10:00, 2:00, and 4:00 each day of that week; drop by at your convenience.

We will issue each of you your first cassette and bill your department accordingly. Each time you turn in a taped cassette to the Word Processing Center for transcription, you will receive a replacement at no cost. If you need a recorder for use away from the office, you must get approval from the appropriate manager.

The equipment will transcribe from either standard or microcassettes, but not from the minicassettes. Although the minicassette capability would be an asset, we want to avoid this additional cost at the present time.

◆ ◆ ◆

Subject: Special Travel Service and Discount from Continental Hotels

We've been able to secure a special reduced corporate rate at the Continental Hotels chain, a discount unavailable through any other local agency at this time. In order to receive this discount, however, we must make all travel arrangements through one company representative.

Ms. Sue Lemitz, suite 4882-D, will be handling this new service for you and dealing directly with Continental. To make your travel arrangements, please call her (ext. 115) with the following information: guest name, department, office location, arrival date, departure date, local and destination contact name and phone number, type of room required (single, double, suite).

100 INTRODUCTIONS

All rooms will be guaranteed for late arrivals. Since Continental will deal with no one other than our designated representative, Ms. Lemitz must make all cancellations or changes for you before she leaves each day at 5:30 p.m. Please make every effort to phone her about a change of plans before that hour; otherwise, the company must pay for any unused room.

◆ ◆ ◆

Subject: New Form for Journal Entries of Manual Invoices and Other Receivables

Attached is a completed sample of the new form designed for journal entries of manual invoices and other receivables. The new form has been changed to provide adequate information for direct feed into the new MARC system.

The major change (circled in red) on the form is the accounts-receivable information section added to the right of the amount columns. The business area coding has been added as a permanent code for data-entry purposes.

This new form should be used only when a receivable entry is being recorded. These new columns, completed only if the receivable entry is a credit and clears a specific open item, will reference the original invoice date and number being credited.

If you have any questions about completing these forms, please notify Bill White at ext. 321.

Do's

- Introduce the person, product, equipment, service, or form immediately.
- Explain how the new product, service, equipment, or form differs from whatever is already available: Is it less expensive? Easier to use? More accurate? Safer? State exactly what its significance is.
- Mention any exceptions to primary application. Who is ineligible to use this service, product, form, equipment? What are its limitations? What perhaps assumed function will it not perform?
- Make the item or service easy to investigate. Most readers approach anything new with a wait-and-see-what-everybody-else-thinks hesitancy. Consider offering a sample; an attached illustration; a "case study" explanation; a demonstration; a class; readily available assistance by phone, visit, or display.
- Use the term "new" or its equivalent in the subject line to call immediate attention.

● When introducing an employee, add a personal touch. Such introductions lean to the unimaginative—assignment, credentials, chain of command. To give staff members a start in conversation, mention a few personal details of both "official" and "unofficial" nature. Be sure, of course, to clear those details with the employee.

INVESTIGATIONS

Weak Model

Subject: Crankcase Explosion, Beston Engine 0990

At approximately 2:30 a.m. on December 30, 198-, Beston Engine 0990 went down due to a crankcase explosion. On Monday, January 1, the maintenance crew pulled all crankcase doors to inspect the cylinders for problems. No solution could be reached, so compression on all cylinders was checked. It was found that the left-hand #4 cylinder had only four pounds of test pressure as opposed to 18 to 20 pounds on all other cylinders. It was then decided to pull the left-hand #4 piston and to inspect the piston and cylinder. The piston was found to be cracked about halfway around at the middle. The rings were stuck and scored. There was a small crack found in the seat area of the air-starting valve in the head, but no water leakage. It was then decided to replace the cylinder, piston, and head. The oil and oil filters were also changed.

The actual cause of the problem was not fully determined. The lubricator to this cylinder was working properly. There was a place at the top of the cylinder liner where the liner separated about .015" from the cylinder body. This separation could have allowed water to get into the cylinder, causing the piston to stick momentarily.

Work on engine 0990 was completed on January 5, 198-, and it was returned to service.

If further information is needed, please advise.

Don'ts _____

   ● Don't use chronological order for details—the suspense format of how you investigated. Instead, distill and report first the essence of your discovery and your recommendation.
   ● Don't shroud your details in the passive voice in an effort to sound "official." If you are authorized by your company to investigate, your report will be official. Active voice and a few pronouns ("we decided to replace . . ." vs. "it was decided to replace . . .") will breathe life into your writing.

Good Models

Subject: System Disc Crash

On July 8, 198-, we had a physical crash of the read/write heads on our oldest disc drive, the first such occurrence in the four-year life of our system. The cause of the problem was a dirty disc pack and infrequent preventive maintenance on the system.

As a result of the crash, we have a damaged disc pack and have had to replace 6 of 20 heads on the drive. Time for repair and recovery amounted to 15 hours.

I have contacted Chilton Company for their recommendations to prevent future occurrences and plan to take advantage of their suggestions:
* Preventive maintenance--Bordelon, out of Phoenix, will provide on-site inspection and cleaning of our packs twice a year at a cost of $16 per pack.
* Damaged pack--Marceau Computer Services will revamp our damaged pack at its main laboratory here in the city for a cost of $390. (A new pack, costing approximately $1,600, will be unnecessary.)

We fully expect that these new measures will prevent reoccurrence of the problem.

◆ ◆ ◆

Subject: Shooting Incident at Belford Plant

On August 4, 198-, at 11:36 p.m., someone fired two 6mm rounds from close range outside the Belford plant gate. One of the three security employees was hit in the arm; after hospital treatment of the minor wound, he was released. We notified the Sheriff's Office and filed a report, but to date there have been no arrests and no shell cases recovered.

Since we know of no such previous incidents, we have made no changes in the site's security as of this time. Nor do we know of changes that would prevent reoccurrence of a similar incident.

An inspection of the gunshot damage revealed that one round hit the south end of the compressor building, entering approximately 10″ above and to the right of the door. The second round hit the north end of the same building, deforming the exterior sheeting adjacent to the exhaust stack.

The two other security employees on duty sighted a white car, model undetermined, leaving the vicinity of the front gate immediately after the shots were fired.

Do's

• The message statement should contain a brief recap of what happened, with what results, and why. Following the basic message, mention recommendations—or possibly action already taken—to prevent a reoccurrence. Finally, follow with details about your actual investigation procedures and specific findings.

• Include the cause or probable cause of the incident upfront. If cause cannot be determined, say so.

• Specify if this is a one-time, infrequent, or recurrent incident. Such information would suggest stronger-than-normal preventive measures, replacement of equipment, or revised procedures.

• Include, if significant and possible, time and dollar loss.

• Be careful that details are exact and plentiful. Your report may later be the basis of legal action.

• Identify subjective statements as such, distinguishing them from investigative facts. Note in the model, "Nor do we know of changes . . ." The writer doesn't say there are no ways to prevent reoccurrence of the incident.

INVITATIONS

Good Models

Subject: Lunch Invitation

Vincent,

Would you be free for lunch with me on Tuesday, August 14? I'll be touring your building on that day and would like for you to be my guest at Regi's Palazzio. Since reservations are sometimes a problem there, please let me know by this Friday if you can make it.

If the date is convenient for you, I plan to ask Jim Andrews to join us. I'd really like for us seriously to consider "pitching" our reorganizational ideas to the right "powers that be."

Looking forward to hearing from you.

Subject: Invitation to July BDS Program

You are invited to attend our July 8, 198-, BDS luncheon and program entitled "Tour Security" to be presented aboard the tour ship <u>Manhattan</u>.

You must make reservations by calling Sharon Rynn at extension 236 by Thursday, July 3. Those who have reservations but do not cancel by 4:00 p.m. July 3 will be billed for the luncheon. Reservations will be limited, so please call early.

Lunch ($7/person, payable at the meeting) will begin at 11:30, followed by a brief discussion of chapter business and then a tour of the ship with presentations from three members of the security staff. The tour and presentations should be concluded by 2:00 p.m.; however, those of you who are interested may remain for the short question-and-answer period.

A map/information sheet is attached for your convenience in finding the tour ship's location. We look forward to seeing you at this unique and informative July program.

Subject: Service-Awards Dinner Invitation

On Thursday, June 6, there will be a service-awards dinner at the Ryan Country Club, 21234 Laneview Drive. One of your staff, Barbara Novak, will be honored this year on her tenth anniversary with the company.

Please let me know if you can be present to make the award to Ms. Novak. We'll need your reservation and those of others in your department who would like to attend, by Tuesday, June 4.

◆   ◆   ◆

Subject: Invitation to Speak at the May 14 Computer Walk-through

Would you schedule us a favor? We'd like you to make a presentation at our May 14 Computer Walk-through in the computer room, tenth floor. Your one-hour (8:00-9:00 a.m.) talk on basic computer terminology, capabilities, and limitations will provide background for the remainder of the day's activities.

If you would agree to conduct the presentation, please phone me by Thursday, April 22.

If you agree to speak, your audience will be primarily the 25 field operators assigned to our Omaha branches. The room will be adequate for seating and will allow "milling around" to examine the equipment. Any visuals you may want to use will need to be projected large enough to be seen from a distance of 40 feet. Also, we'd like you to allow about 15 minutes at the end of your talk for audience questions. After your presentation, Bill Waddel and Tim Johnson will be leading the group through the area; please feel free to contact them about any "groundwork" they'd like you to lay.

You are welcome to come early at 7:30 to have coffee and donuts with the group during their get-acquainted period and to stay after your presentation and join other activities.

Should you need any help in setup arrangements or in reserving audiovisual equipment, contact my assistant Muriel Brown at extension 550. In my absence, Muriel will also be glad to answer questions about the content expectations, format, or audience.

Do's _____

    ● Mention the event and/or occasion immediately: retirement dinner for Chuck Normont, monthly business meeting, or lunch discussion of relocation plans.

● Request a reply by a certain date, not "as soon as possible" or some other vague time.

● Consider all details such as date, time, place, cost, reservations (state if or if not required), map or travel directions, contact name, and number for more information. When you're inviting someone to speak, mention specific topic guidelines, time length, other speakers and their topics, question-and-answer period, equipment needs, audience type and size, expenses or honorarium, and any follow-up expected.

● Give the agenda. Remember that readers may make a decision about attendance solely on the basis of the program or meeting information given in your memo. Also, the agenda gives necessary information for those who may have to come late or leave early; they can decide if attending only a portion of the event would be worthwhile. Even in a personal luncheon invitation, agenda or "purpose" details allow your reader to think beforehand so that your discussion is productive.

JOB DESCRIPTIONS

Good Models

Position--Technical Assistant
Ad Valorem Tax Department

Summary: The Technical Assistant, Ad Valorem Tax Department, maintains tax records and provides information to the Property Tax Department and Governmental Compliance section of the Legal Department for inclusion in their reports.

Reports to: Supervisor, Ad Valorem Tax Department

Qualifications: Two years' college

Responsibilities

1. Supplies to the Director of the Property Tax Department an annual account of all Greenhill pipelines that encroach upon any and all taxing districts within each county in this state.
2. Informs the Director of the Property Tax Department of the county and taxing districts in which all Greenhill fee properties are located.
3. Furnishes to the Director of the Property Tax Department all necessary information for the annual tax reports such as the following: Barrett County Average Age Study, Construction Materials Inventory, Plant and Structures Annual Report, Annual Budget Forecast.
4. Provides the Supervisor of the Government Compliance section of the Legal Department with any information required for formulating reports necessary to his function.

Records to Be Maintained
to Carry Out the Above Responsibilities

* County files
* County-fee and surface-lease files
* Property-ownership maps
* Gathering maps
* Tax ledgers
* Major-equipment ledgers
* Computerized database of all taxing information

◆ ◆ ◆

Position--Equipment Technician

Summary: The Equipment Technician is responsible for equipment maintenance and repair and for keeping related records. Also, he recommends changes in equipment to improve reliability, increase capability, and/or reduce maintenance costs.

Reports to: Maintenance Supervisor

Qualifications:
* High-school graduate
* Trade school or two years' technical school
* Two years' experience as journeyman in related skills, such as machine repair or electrical work

Responsibilities:
* Diagnoses equipment operating problems and makes required repairs
* Performs preventive maintenance
* Makes recommendations concerning machine replacement or modifications to lower maintenance costs and/or improve capabilities
* Establishes and maintains spare-parts inventory
* Keeps up-to-date records of all equipment drawings, specifications, parts, and addresses of manufacturers
* Keeps records on each machine, listing proper maintenance procedures and dates of maintenance and repairs

Do's _____

● Begin with a summary statement of overall responsibilities.

● Be broad enough so that the job description can be tailored to fit a variety of locations or performance standards. That does not mean, however, to revert to abstractions. In other words, in writing a job description for a sales field representative, you cannot say, "shall make at least ten calls per month on new accounts." In some territories that require extensive traveling between accounts, ten such calls may involve 70 percent of a salesperson's time, while in other areas ten calls might involve only two days' work. Instead, give a broad (yet concrete) description of performance standards, saying, for instance, that 15 percent of all sales calls should involve prospective clients. For some employees that may mean two calls per month; for others that may mean ten.

● Organize specific tasks into broad categories of responsibilities.

● State responsibilities in measurable terms. Avoid comments such as, "Initiates effective publicity for new services and products." What is "effective publicity"? Or, "Is responsible for maintaining positive company image with the community." How? When? By whose standards? Instead, refer to actions to be performed and measured: "Holds monthly staff meetings to improve coordination of efforts." "Reports all budget expenditures over $500." "Creates individualized patient-care plans on all assigned patients."

● Mention to whom the employee reports in each area of responsibility if the chain of command is unclear. This is particularly important if the job involves work for several people or if the position is primarily a liaison between departments.

● Show how individual duties relate to others' responsibilities within the department and outside the department, if appropriate. For instance, in the job description for the equipment technician, notice in the second sentence that "he recommends"; in other words, this position does not hold final authority in the areas listed.

● Include sources of information needed to perform the job.

● Use headings and lists. Keep wording brief, as on a resume.

LEGAL OPINIONS

Weak Model

Subject: Liability Under the Farnsworth Contract

Tundrell's liability under the Farnsworth contract is only to the named insured and such parties included under the definition of insured in the policy and only for actual loss incurred in reliance thereon in undertaking good faith (a) to comply with the requirements thereof, or (b) to eliminate exceptions shown in attached Schedule B, or (c) to acquire or create the estate of interest or mortgage covered by said commitment. In no event does Tundrell's liability exceed the amount stated in the attached Schedule A for the policy, and such liability is subject to the insuring provisions, exclusions from coverage, and the conditions and stipulations of the policy in favor of the insured that were thereby incorporated by reference and were made a part of that commitment except as expressly modified therein.

Any claim of loss or damage, whether or not based on negligence, and that arises out of the status of the title to the estate of interest or the lien of the insured mortgage covered or any action asserting such claim, is restricted to the provisions, conditions, and stipulations of the contract.

If you have other questions about our liability, please advise.

Don'ts

   ● Don't lapse into gibberish intelligible only to your occupational species.
   ● Don't write in the abstract—to "Everyman." Picture your readers and write to them as you would explain the situation for their specific applications.
   ● Don't bury important ideas in long sentences and paragraphs.
   ● Don't simply restate a law or contract's wording: Make application to the questions at hand.
   ● Don't make your reader look elsewhere for details to understand the basic message. For example, the memo writer above continually alludes to other documents.
   ● Don't be wordy. Cut these legalisms from your memo: redundant synonyms (last will and testament, maintenance and upkeep, null and void); ready-made introductions that could fit onto any number of opinions on the same subject matter; unnecessary quotes that you could paraphrase; formalisms (party of the first part); plain old everyday repetition.

Good Models

Subject: Liability Under the Farnsworth Contract

Tundrell's liability under the Farnsworth contract is only to Farnsworth, not subsequent buyers such as Sibbo. Furthermore, we are liable to Farnsworth only for the actual loss caused by their relying on our initial commitment; that liability amounts to $226,000 to date. Such reliance involves their legal battles with Belasco County, as explained on the attachment.

I suggest we draft a letter to Sibbo explaining our position and then settle with Farnsworth for the $226,000. If you agree, let me know and I'll proceed with the proper paperwork.

◆ ◆ ◆

Subject: Lease No. 876-44-4468, Recinda Prospect, Bellview County, KB Tracts 35, 37, 38, and 40

To summarize my lengthy opinion (attached) on the Recinda Prospect: Although there is no clear authority established in the state courts, the lease in Bellview County is maintained. Additionally, as a precautionary measure, we should execute a new lease in which the wording would clarify earlier vague issues. The effective data should be the same as the prior lease date.

All parties would benefit, and all are agreeable to write this new lease.

If you would like further research into the matter, please let me know.

◆ ◆ ◆

Subject: Exemptions of Fair Labor Standards Act

You raised the question whether the Fair Labor Standards Act and the wages and hours provisions therein apply to our inspectors who perform services outside U.S. territorial waters.

My answer: If an otherwise nonexempt inspector performs services outside U.S. territorial waters for an <u>entire</u> workweek, he is exempt from the Act <u>for that workweek</u>. If, on the other hand, the inspector performs services within the United States for <u>any portion</u> of a given workweek, he remains nonexempt for that entire workweek.

The term "workweek" is defined as follows:

An employee's workweek is a fixed and regularly recurring period of 168 hours—seven consecutive 24-hour periods. It need not coincide with the calendar week but may begin on any day and at any hour of the day. For purposes of computing pay due under the Fair Labor Standards Act, a single workweek may be established for a plant or other establishment as a whole, or different workweeks may be established for different employees or groups of employees. Once the beginning time of an employee's workweek is established, it remains fixed regardless of the schedule of hours worked by him. The beginning of the workweek may be changed if the change is intended to be permanent and is not designed to evade the overtime requirements of the Act. (Dept. of Labor Interpretive Bulletin, 29 C.F.R. §778.105)

Exemptions
The act provides for several exemptions, including the following:

The provisions of sections 206 [re: minimum wages], 207 [re: maximum hours, i.e., overtime], 211 [re: collection of data] and 212 [re: child labor] of this title shall not apply with respect to any employee whose services during the workweek are performed in a workplace within a foreign country or within territory under the jurisdiction of the United States other than the following: the District of Columbia; Puerto Rico; the Virgin Islands, outer Continental Shelf lands defined in the Outer Continental Shelf Lands Act; American Samoa; Guam; Wake Island; Eniwetok Atoll; Kwajalein Atoll; Johnston Island; a State of the United States. Id. §213 (f).

The Act does not apply outside the United States; accordingly, an inspector who performs services in a foreign country is exempt from the Act for the purposes of those services.

Case Law Support
* Burns v. Metcalfe Construction Company, 69 F. Supp. 381, 382 (W.D. Mo. 1946): The Act held inapplicable to construction work performed in Canada.
* Bernhard v. Metcalfe Construction Company, 64 F. Supp. 953, 954 (D. Neb. 1946): The application of the Act held to be limited to "the territorial limits of the United States, its territories and possessions."
* Filardo v. Foley Bros., Inc., 181 Misc. 136, 45 N.Y.S.2d 262, 263–64 (Sup. Ct. 1943): The Act held inapplicable "to work and employees in foreign countries even though such employees are citizens of the United States."
* Wirtz v. Healy, 227 F. Supp. 123 (N.D. Ill. 1964): The Act held inapplicable to workweek "in which the tour escort performs all of his work exclusively in a foreign country."

This case further refines the principle of the Act as stated in my second paragraph of this memo:

> The exemption provided by Section 13 (f) of the Act is inapplicable to a tour escort of defendants who, during a particular workweek, performs services both in a workplace within the United States and in a workplace within a foreign country. . . . Thus, when a tour escort of defendants spends part of workweek with a tour in the United States, it makes no difference where the remainder of such work in that week is performed; the tour escort is entitled to the benefits of the Act for the entire week. . . .
>
> The exemption provided by Section 13 (f) of the Act is applicable to a tour escort of defendants during any workweek in which the tour escort performs all of his work exclusively in a foreign country. (Id. at 129)

Illustration of Our Application

For an example of the Act as it would apply to Helco: Assume that the workweek for both Inspector A and Inspector B begins and terminates on Sunday at midnight. Inspector A leaves the United States on Wednesday of week 1 to investigate a construction site in England and returns on Wednesday of week 2. Since Inspector A performs services within the United States during parts of both week 1 and week 2, the Act applies to him for both of the weeks, including the time spent in England. He must be paid minimum wage and overtime.

Inspector B leaves the United States on Wednesday of week 1 to investigate a construction site in England and returns on Wednesday of week 3. Since Inspector B performs services within the United States during parts of week 1 and week 3, the Act applies to him with respect to those two weeks, including the time spent in England during those two weeks. But, since Inspector B performs services exclusively outside the United States during week 2, the Act would not apply to that week. He could be paid less than minimum wage and receive no overtime pay for services during that second week in England.

I hope this clarifies our situation. If there is anything further, let me know.

Do's

- Either give the summary of your opinion at the beginning of the technical explanation or include it in a transmittal letter. If there is any action to be taken, recommend it upfront.
- If it is necessary to use unfamiliar legal terms when writing to lay readers, explain such terms the first time they appear.
- Pay particular attention to sentence and paragraph length to keep your writing readable. Contrary to popular belief among lawyers, periods do not

create loopholes; with good transitional words and phrases, you can lead your reader into the next sentence or paragraph for further elaboration, exceptions, or qualifications. Short paragraphs also provide eye relief and call attention to significant ideas.

- Use examples to make vague or difficult concepts more understandable.

- Put all important information in the text body, not in footnotes or attachments. In the Fair Labor Standards Act memo, note the placement of the workweek definition and other case support as part of the text body.

- Use informative headings for a lengthy text.

MEETINGS, TO ANNOUNCE

Good Model

Subject: Barbarina Isle Project Meeting

I have scheduled a meeting of the task force for developing the Barbarina Isle Project for September 6 at 10:00 a.m. in my office. Because of the unusual technical problems that have come to light in the past few days, we need to discuss the issues below.

Please note what individual preparation you should make before the meeting. If for any reason you cannot attend or gather the required information, let me know immediately (ext. 682) so that I can reschedule for later in the week.

Agenda

1.	What is the cost of additional technical personnel to solve the problems?	(individual reports on projected costs)	5 min.
2.	Can the problems possibly be identified as "projects" for which actual costs can be recaptured?	(open discussion)	30 min.
3.	Will the owners resist approval of these new "problem/project" costs? If so, what approach can we take to sell them? Who should do the selling?	(John Davis and Fred Qupo will report on previous "feeler" conversations with the owners; open discussion to follow)	1 hour

If for some reason we have not come to conclusions by noon, we'll have lunch brought in--that is, if any of you can eat with this bugaboo still hanging over our heads!

Do's _____

● State when you have scheduled the meeting. Other brief details such as where, what time, and why can usually be given in one "message" statement.

● Ask for confirmation of attendance so that if key people will be unable to attend or if necessary information is unavailable, you can reschedule. Better to cancel than conduct meaningless meetings.

● Include the meeting agenda in question form so that attendees know specifically which direction their thought, planning, and comments should take. Generally stated topics such as "technical problems" give few clues for attendees to come prepared with data, questions, or comments. Also, include time allocations for agenda items. Although these cannot always be adhered to, stated guidelines help attendees to know the depth of discussion expected and later to keep the meeting from getting bogged down in insignificant detail. Also, time limits and the order of agenda will allow those whose presence is not required for the entire meeting to come late or leave early.

- Give any premeeting assignments to speed the meeting's progress.

MEETINGS, TO DECLINE

Good Model

Subject: Absence at Public-Relations Meeting

I will be unable to attend the upcoming public-relations committee meeting to be held Friday, May 8, at the Merrimac in Dallas. Due to my recent heart ailment, my physician has restricted my work schedule to three hours a day and has advised me not to travel.

I'll be in touch with Alice Henry, however, after May 8 to catch up on discussion and decisions made in my absence.

Enclosed you will find my nominations for the upcoming scholarships our branch would like to offer. Also, I'm returning my marked ballot for the STA election.

Best wishes for a productive meeting.

Do's

- State your nonattendance at the meeting immediately. Be sure to include all, or at least some relevant time, place, or purpose details so that your reader is not confused about which meeting.
- Notify the appropriate person *in advance* about your absence. If you are to play an important part in the meeting, others may decide to reschedule.
- Give legitimate reasons for your nonattendance. Such information will tell the scheduler whether a postponement would be in order. If you simply don't have the time or don't see the need to attend, say so; if appropriate, offer to send a representative.
- State your plans for following up on the meeting results.
- Forward any information or report on any action necessary for the meeting discussion.

MEETINGS, TO RECORD MINUTES

Good Model

Subject: Minutes of the December 8 Safety Meeting

The third safety meeting, held December 8, 198-, focused on establishing a new Accident Investigation Committee, companywide publicity efforts, and verbal accident reporting:

Establishment of Accident Investigation Committees
By January 15, management will appoint 12 employees from each site as an "accident investigation pool." When an accident occurs, the district manager will notify three people from this pool to investigate and report as follows:

* They will contact any injured employees, any witnesses of the accident, and the supervisor at the job site to gather information on causes, responsibility, and prevention.
* They will make a written report of their findings to the district manager (a copy to the safety coordinator) within three working days after the accident.
* The district manager will forward his report and any recommendations for disciplinary action to the appropriate senior vice president within ten working days.

Publicity Focus and Visuals
We agreed that the primary focus of all publicity should be to make supervisors realize they are responsible for the safety of all employees under their supervision.

* Bulletin board posters showing the number of accident-free days have been displayed in all divisions.
* Floyd Mayhen suggested and will take responsibility to see that large safety banners be posted in all field offices.

New Requirements for Verbal Reporting of Accidents
Any employee involved in an accident, along with his supervisor, will be required to meet with the safety division at its next scheduled session to present the circumstances of the accident, to report on lost time, and to recommend preventive measures.

Miscellaneous
1. We agreed to change the safety-meeting format on occasion to allow for field-related topic presentations by members of the group.
2. We discussed the possibility of filming "staged" accidents as the basis for future safety programs. No conclusion was reached.

FOLLOW-UP ASSIGNMENTS

1. Floyd Mayhen will investigate costs and design of safety banners and bring a recommendation for the next meeting.
2. Dusty Miller will notify appropriate managers about their appointing a 12-member "accident investigation pool" at each site.
3. Bonnie Tipps will draft the discussed procedures for distribution to the "accident investigation pools."

Those attending the meeting were Abe Force, Julia Benhan, Floyd Mayhen, Dusty Miller, Bonnie Tipps, Henry Armory, and Kate Hendrix.

Do's

- Briefly state the major topics of discussion or meeting conclusions upfront. However, delay mentioning specific assignments until after you have recorded the essence of each topic discussion.
- Use headings to help multiple readers focus on agenda items of individual interest. On occasion, you may want to use your discussion questions as headings and then record your conclusions and decisions in list form.
- Remember that space given to recording a topic discussion suggests its importance; don't get carried away with minutiae. You'll have to avoid the once-upon-a-time detail that always surrounds each discussion topic and focus on the major problems identified or solved, the major questions raised or answered, and results and/or related follow-up action.
- Arrange topics in most-to-least significant format rather than in order of discussion.
- Include specific follow-up assignments—who should do what by when.
- Include names of attendees last.

"NO" REPLIES

Weak Model

[Subordinate has requested approval to install new control title-policy procedures.]

Subject: Programming of New Procedures to Control Title Policies

In your memo of June 22, you stated that Mike Francis is studying how to install a procedure to control title policies by February 198-. Why are you following through on this idea without my approval? I'd like to understand how many man-hours it would take to install such a system, both the programming and whatnot, and then I'd like to understand how many hours a year would be required to maintain such a system.

I'm very concerned that we don't have people who are checking on people who are checking on people. It has always been our policy to maintain offices where one person performs and controls all functions.

I have asked Mic Lakeland to make a study of all policies being sent to Pittsburgh and to decide which of these might be eliminated. This study came to mind when I found that Florida is sending policies, the guaranty register, and a check to Pittsburgh. However, Atlanta, Dowdent, and scores of other offices do not send title policies to this Pittsburgh office. If we are well controlled, Florida should be eliminated as well as other offices, unless there is some overriding reason. I was pleasantly surprised to see that First American of Oregon had received orders to stop having any independent agents send policies to them.

In paragraph six of your memo you state that we do have instructions to offices to send in and get reinsurance on anything in excess of $5 million. We also have instructions that they get approval for policies less than that. I don't understand why we need any additional procedures. I believe our losses are going to come more from failure to follow procedures, such as paying off previous liens, than from issuing policies over $5 million without the reinsurance. I maintain that we have "implemented procedures" to determine that we do not issue policies over $5 million without being reinsured. But I don't see why these have to be on computer. The mere fact that we have instructed people not to write policies over $5 million without reinsurance should be adequate procedure, as with all other instructions.

Don'ts

- Don't use the basic functional format. A "no" reply requires special arrangement; you must give the reader time to adjust to what's coming.
- Don't begin on a negative tone. Notice how the question "Why are you following through on this idea without my approval?" sets a reprimanding note for the remainder of the memo.
- Don't hide behind "company policy" or a that's-the-way-we've-always-done-it explanation. Even if company policy or past experience is a valid basis for your response, explain the reasoning behind the policy or past action.
- Don't give a patronizing lecture about how things should be or state obvious platitudes. Look at the last sentence of the memo; of course all instructions should be followed, but are they always? Watch admonitions such as, "We should not incur any unnecessary expenses." Who should?
- Don't be wishy-washy with your answer. In this memo, the "no" comes between the lines. The writer asks for information on how many man-hours the installation and maintenance would require; then later he seems to be saying the new procedures are unnecessary. Is he really saying, "No, don't proceed"? Or is he saying, "I want more information before I approve"? Notice other equally wishy-washy wording: "unless there is some overriding reason," "it would seem to me," "I don't understand why we need any additional procedures," "I maintain that," "but I don't see why these have to be on computer."
- Don't get sidetracked in discussing other issues to which you object; leave those for a later memo.

Good Models

[Subordinate has requested approval to install new control title-policy procedures.]

Subject: Programming of New Procedures to Control Title Policies

In reviewing your memo of June 22, I noted that Mike Francis is attempting to install a procedure to control title policies by February 198-. I'm very concerned that we don't have people who are checking on people who are checking on people. I prefer offices where one person performs and controls all functions. Such autonomy creates variety on the job and helps fix responsibility for outstanding achievement.

I have asked Mic Lakeland to make a study of all policies being sent to Pittsburgh and to decide which of these might be eliminated. Other of our branch offices such as Atlanta, Dowdent, and even our competitors (First American of Oregon) have cut overhead by eliminating such unnecessary distributions and checks. Also, as stated in paragraph six of your memo, we already have procedures to handle reinsurance on anything in excess of $5 million. We also have procedures to get approval for policies written for less than that.

I believe losses are going to come more from failure to follow existing procedures, such as paying off previous liens, than from issuing policies over $5 million without the reinsurance. Therefore, I do not think programming new control procedures would be appropriate or cost-effective at this time.

I do appreciate your attention to detail, however; if we do have branches that are not following these already-written instructions, please point that out to me.

Join me in cutting out some of the paperwork. Thanks.

◆ ◆ ◆

[Subordinate has suggested that closing meetings be eliminated.]

Subject: Monthly Closing Meetings

Bill, I received your note about the last closing meeting. Although the meeting you attended may not have been as productive as we all would have liked, we are all attempting to identify and resolve problems associated with this area of responsibility. To do this, we need the insight and cooperation of MIS and of all the accounting units; therefore, I feel that to eliminate completely the closing meetings would be premature at this time.

But let me assure you that we are trying to make the format as productive as possible. And as encouragement for the future, let me emphasize that when all the closing structure falls into place, we likely will have no further need for these meetings.

I appreciate your interest in the closing project, and please continue to advise me of any other concerns about our progress.

◆ ◆ ◆

[Subordinate has requested funds for a grinding upgrade team.]

Subject: Grinding Upgrade Team

After our Thursday discussion about establishing a grinding upgrade team, I have reevaluated our ability to support such an effort in fiscal 198-.

Current budget and planning includes an extensive press rebuild and general upgrade program and also a rebuild of one of the roughing grinders. In view of these previously established programs, of limited maintenance technicians and engineering staff, and of existing budget planning, to approve your project will be impossible at this time. I do not question your evaluation of the need for this upgrading; I simply must compare it to priorities of other programs already budgeted for this year.

Please keep me informed on other important phases of your work. We do want to remain as flexible as possible as priorities change.

Do's

● Begin on a positive, or at least neutral, note—even if simply a re-statement of the request or assurance that you have carefully studied the situation. The "bottom-line" message in a "no" reply should not come upfront because it hits the reader too hard; some audiences would not even bother to read your following explanation.

● Build up with reasons for your forthcoming "no." In this fashion, you are asking the reader to examine the evidence with you and to accept your reasoning and conclusion. Don't prolong the explanations to the point that you sound defensive or pleading; however, don't make your explanations so brief and general as to be unconvincing.

● Make a firm statement of your "no" answer.

● Mention any conditions under which you will reconsider—for example, "when priorities change," "when business improves," or "if we have branches not following these procedures."

● Offer any alternative "yes" willingly, not begrudgingly. Notice that in the memo on monthly closing meetings, the writer promises to make the format as productive as possible and possibly to eliminate the meetings altogether at a later date.

● End on a positive note. At least thank the reader for his interest or effort. Leave him with a back-to-business-as-usual feeling.

OBJECTIVES

Good Models

Subject: Objectives for Calendar Year 198-

Renew or Cancel Out-of-Date Blanket Orders
I plan to review the names of authorized personnel who issue blanket
orders and to identify evergreens, year-to-year, or annual orders. These
orders will be renewed or canceled.

Draft Procedures as Office-Services Handout
Procedures will include the following: definition of blanket order, benefits,
appropriate items for blanket orders, types of orders, releases.

Establish New Filing System
We will set up a more convenient filing system to alert us to expiring
blanket orders so that proper action (renewal, price increases or reductions,
bid solicitation, cancellation) can be taken without delay.

Study Cost-Effectiveness
We will identify our dependable suppliers and encourage them, while
weeding out the undependable ones (vendors who promise but don't
deliver, overship or undership consistently, ship substitute goods, are
continually unavailable by phone). Additionally, we will search for backup
suppliers on existing sole-source items. Finally, we intend to take
advantage of corporate national agreements where advantageous.

Conduct Regular Staff Meetings
We plan to meet informally twice a month to educate each other on
sources, references, and problems in an effort to improve overall
production and efficiency.

◆ ◆ ◆

Subject: Activity Plan, 198-

Our primary objective for fiscal 198- is to introduce computers to the
midwestern branches, specifically Glennora, Hallsville, Mid City, Foster,
Planter, and Holister. Trips are planned to all these locations within the
next month so that we may see what each has accomplished toward this
objective. In addition, I have planned to meet with Joseph Tidas, who has
written three computer books and will, I'm sure, have valuable ideas for
us.

Specifically, I've outlined six objectives in order of priority:
* Introduce computers to six of our branches
* Complete the programming here in our corporate office
* Reduce property taxes by $160,000
* Employ a national management consulting firm by September
* Establish controls on report reproduction and reduce costs by $5,000
* Improve the format and detail of financial analysis provided to corporate each month

I look forward to the upcoming year and progress toward these goals.

Do's

• State the objectives in measurable goals; include dollars and dates where possible. Be specific in your verb choice: Will you review, identify, research, improve, reduce, draft, implement, eliminate? If you "improve" something, to what extent? If you "review" something, what do you plan to look for and do afterward? In other words, at the end of the activity-plan period, you and your supervisor should be able to review this memo and measure what you have accomplished toward these goals.

• Use headings and listings, rather than paragraph form exclusively, to aid a skimming reader in overviewing the total plan. If you intend to focus on only one major product, break it down into steps, stages, or results expected.

• List objectives in descending order of importance or by dates to be accomplished.

PERFORMANCE APPRAISALS
(for appraisals recommending termination, see "Dismissals")

Weak Model

Subject: Evaluation of Performance--Sharon Hyatt

Sharon Hyatt, hired June 28, 198-, as instructor for employee-orientation seminars, shows an amiable disposition toward her instructor duties and toward employees attending her seminars, but those same interpersonal skills need application in the Training Department. With her co-workers, Sharon seems reluctant to participate in planning and shows little willingness to assume responsibilities outside her sphere of orientation work.

Reaction sheets at the end of her orientation seminars suggest that Sharon has satisfactory stand-up presentation skills and has designed an effective curriculum; but, of course, new employees will always be reluctant to evaluate negatively their first company instructor.

Now that the design of the seminar has been concluded and actual presentation and travel time takes only about 10 working days of the month, Sharon will need to assume additional training duties such as audiovisual scripts and workbook materials for courses designed by other instructors. To date, Sharon has little background in this area (a fact we knew when she was hired) and demonstrates reluctance in assuming these graphic and writing assignments. Not surprisingly, resentment among other trainers about her "I-can't-do" attitude has created departmental tension. Two discussions with Sharon about this reluctance "to get her hands dirty" with actual production of curriculum materials have resulted in very little improvement.

Sharon's professionalism in the classroom, including dress and projection of company image, is, as always, quite acceptable. She deals well with departmental supervisors and managers in her scheduling and expense reporting efforts.

Don'ts

• Don't use the "sandwich" technique of organization—that is, don't sandwich a strength between two weaknesses or vice versa. This way, the reader finds it hard to "keep score" on overall performance. In either paragraph or list form, divide the strengths and weaknesses/needs so that they all get maximum attention.

- Don't end statements of good performance with "but" clauses. Not: "Martha shows much skill in dealing with the public in person, *but* her telephone technique seems abrupt and abrasive." You'll notice that the last clause detracts from or cancels out the first, positive statement. Note the effect of the first statement in the previous memo.

- Don't list strengths and weaknesses without making a judgment about whether this employee should be terminated, whether corrective action can be taken, whether he or she should be promoted or given increased responsibilities. In this memo, what exactly is the evaluator saying? Should Sharon be terminated? Given training in scripting and writing skills? Reassigned to new seminar delivery responsibilities so that she can use her presentation skills full-time?

- Don't be general about qualitative performance or improvements needed. Vague words often found on performance evaluation forms such as "poor," "satisfactory," or "excellent" report very little, give the employee no idea how to improve, and fail to reveal evaluation standards. If you must use a form for evaluation and must circle one-word judgments, elaborate elsewhere on the form or by attachment. State, for instance, that the employee's punctuality record shows tardies 20 percent of the time and that if this is not cut to less than 2 percent, he can expect termination. That's specific.

- Don't mention salary; salary should never be directly associated with the appraisal process. Someone who performs satisfactorily in all categories may be led to believe that *every* satisfactory or complimentary evaluation will lead to a merit increase. Performance-appraisal "hints" disappoint when such is not the case. Neither would you want to have to fabricate weaknesses as a justification for no salary increase.

Good Models

Subject: Performance Appraisal for Alan Buchannan

Alan Buchannan completed his basic training program four months ago and is progressing as expected in learning his territory. I am pleased with his performance and look forward to increased sales as he gets more experience in presentation techniques. To date, he has sold six copiers and furnished five leads that have resulted in three typewriter sales. Because of his fluency in both English and French, I have hopes of eventually directing him into our International Marketing Division's management training program.

Alan has been conscientious in submitting sales and expense reports by the required deadlines with the appropriate documentation. In all such paperwork, he shows great attention to detail.

His interpersonal skills are excellent. In my visits to his territory, I've noted his instant rapport with clients--the same rapport he has earlier established with his peers at training sessions and monthly meetings.

Alan also demonstrates a conscientious attitude toward work in his long hours (returning phone calls even late into the evening) and his voluminous reading of outside material on competitors' products as well as our own lines.

Closing techniques, one area of needed improvement, will be my primary focus with him in the months to come. He has asked me to accompany him to three of his most difficult accounts and then to offer intensive follow-up critique.

Alan continues to be an asset to our division, and I look forward to helping him increase sales by 15 percent during this next three-month period.

◆ ◆ ◆

Subject: Performance Appraisal--Michael Beane

During the present review period, Michael Beane's performance has been fully satisfactory; his work meets expectations for a qualified and experienced maintenance supervisor. With attention to the developmental needs outlined below, he will become an excellent performer in this position.

Strengths
* Effective supervisory skills: He has been able to determine equipment maintenance and repair priorities. He has managed to schedule support of production equipment and facility needs with a minimum of downtime. He shows complete knowledge of work in progress and can estimate completion dates within a few hours of actual repair.
* Effective cost-control efforts: He has located multiple suppliers for several critical replacement parts, thus reducing long lead time and high shipping costs. Additionally, he has found ways to use in-house skills of his staff to support engineering projects usually requiring outside contract work.
* Excellent equipment knowledge, both mechanical and electrical: This knowledge has contributed to work direction, priority scheduling, and maintenance procedures.

Developmental Needs
* Knowledge of variable and base operating expense budgets, both their planning and control: I plan to arrange a two-day meeting with

all first-line supervisors in my division and discuss with them how Jedmont's business philosophy applies specifically to their job assignments and spending decisions. Then two months after that meeting, Michael and the other supervisors will present me with budget forecasts for next year.

* <u>Improvement in both verbal and written communication skills</u>: I have requested that the Training Department schedule Michael in the first communications seminar available this spring, March 4-7. After this seminar, we'll be working closely in editing interdepartmental memos that go out of his office.

Michael has agreed with these comments, as indicated by his signature below, and is looking forward to another year of improved performance as maintenance supervisor.

Do's

● Summarize the employee's performance at the outset. Then follow with specific strengths and weaknesses/needs. Either list recommended actions or efforts at improvements along with each weakness they are meant to correct, or separate them into a paragraph of "follow-up" action. Include details as you discuss individual strengths or weaknesses/needs.

● Decide about the "status" of the employee and his progress: Do you recommend demotion? Reassignment? Is the employee performing at the level he is expected to maintain without future upward mobility? (This is the status of the maintenance supervisor in the second memo; see the second sentence of that memo.) Should the employee remain in his present position for a longer time before taking on increased responsibility? (This is the status of the salesman in the first memo; see sentences two and four of that memo.) Is the employee ready for increased responsibility now? Does he have significant potential for advancement, and should he be directed into broader responsibility as training for a management position? Remember that the purpose of the appraisal process is to deal with future performance; thus, the content of the appraisal must focus on this satisfactory/unsatisfactory judgment and future courses of action/improvement.

● Make sure the characteristics you judge are relevant to job performance. For example, don't mention interpersonal skills if the job calls for little interaction with other people.

● Evaluate on a representative sample of total job-effectiveness rather than on isolated situations that may happen to stand out in your mind.

● Be specific about criteria for measuring. Notice evaluation standards in the preceding memos: attention to paperwork, long hours, equipment knowledge, little downtime. How much sales increase do you expect in the next period? How many hours of downtime due to unavailable replacement parts are unacceptable?

● Keep the tone nonthreatening. You should sound like a coach rather than a judge—unless, of course, you are recommending dismissal of the employee. Try to state weaknesses in a positive way, such as "improvements needed" or "developmental actions."

• Suggest ways to overcome weaknesses and provide for follow-up on the suggestions and improvements. Keep the words simple and clear; both the evaluator and the employee should be able to understand in concrete terms what and how to improve.

• Get feedback from the employee before writing your appraisal so that you can state his attitude about plans toward improvement or his lack of agreement and cooperation with your designed objectives and measurements. In the first example, the salesman has asked for help on closing techniques, thus showing agreement. In the second example, the employee has signed the memo.

POLICY STATEMENTS

Weak Model

Subject: Policy on Sick Days

Let me remind you that falsifying company records with regard to absence or sickness is a Class "A" Offense. The penalty for such an offense is immediate discharge without prior warning.

In order for you to be paid for sick days, a doctor's excuse must be presented to your immediate supervisor. If your illness is not severe enough to require a doctor's visit, then you may elect to take a vacation day--provided you are entitled to a vacation exceeding one week. If you are not eligible for vacation time longer than one week, you will not be paid for the absence due to sickness without a doctor's excuse.

Don'ts

• Don't state the policy in a negative format and tone. The first paragraph in this memo is a threat rather than a statement of benefit, which sick-pay policy really is. To give this same information in a positive manner, begin the memo, "To be eligible for sick pay, you must present a . . ."; then, as a matter of further information, add a reminder about falsification of records.

Good Models

Subject: Change in Eligibility Requirements for Employee Stock-Purchase Plan

At the November board meeting, the directors of Forbas Manufacturing approved a change in the eligibility requirements for participation in the Employee Stock-Purchase Plan. Effective with the fiscal quarter beginning January 1, 198-, all employees who have completed one year of service with the company (prior policy called for two years of service) will be eligible to join the plan.

The Employee Stock-Purchase Plan is an effective savings plan in which 1,200 Forbas Manufacturing employees are now enrolled. In fact, during the past fiscal year, enrollment has increased 46 percent.

New enrollments for each quarter must be received by the tenth day of the new quarter. Should you have questions about "joining the bandwagon" or if you want to get an enrollment form, contact Liz Smith (ext. 282).

◆ ◆ ◆

Subject: Contributions Policy

Browning Industries desires to make commitments of great and lasting value to society. Our corporate contributions program has been designed to advance the welfare of all its employees, customers, stockholders, and the general public. We intend, particularly, to be a good corporate citizen of the communities in which our employees are located and where the company operates.

Browning Industries will pursue the following general objectives:
* To improve community services and quality of life in areas where the company has employees
* To encourage and improve the quality of our educated labor force
* To support efforts designed to bring all Americans, in particular women, minorities, and the disadvantaged, to equal status in all areas of American life
* To strengthen public confidence in business in general
* To increase goodwill for Browning Industries

Categories of Contributions
The company will contribute to organizations and activities within three areas: health and welfare, education, and civic organizations. The emphasis of each is outlined as follows:

Health and Welfare
This category includes assistance to federated drives such as the United Way, hospitals and medical facilities, youth agencies, recreational organizations, and national health and welfare groups. Our degree of participation in each of these will be determined by the number of our employees in proportion to the local population.

Education
This category includes contributions to educational support organizations, private educational institutions, research, and scholarship funds. Priority will be given to institutions involved in research activities related to company interests.

Civic Organizations
This category includes assistance to programs of community and neighborhood improvement, energy conservation, justice and law, volunteer fire and rescue groups, civic rights and equal opportunity, government administration and reform. and employment and training for

the disadvantaged. Emphasis, again, will be on local programs affecting communities where the company has employees.

General Guidelines for Contributions

Although the company's contributions program will be administered in a flexible manner in response to changing community needs, the general guidelines below will apply:

1. The company prefers to focus its giving through significant contributions (in excess of $300) to key organizations rather than through numerous smaller contributions to many organizations.
2. Contributions are limited to nonprofit organizations exempt from taxation under the Internal Revenue Code.
3. All recipients will operate their programs according to equal-opportunity objectives.
4. Commitments should generally not exceed three years to assure the company's flexibility to changing needs.
5. Requests/proposals for funding should be submitted during the second quarter of the year preceding funding.
6. All solicitations made by phone should be verified in writing.

General Limitations on Contributions

In general, contributions will not be made to the following:

* Churches or other organizations for strictly religious purposes
* Veterans' or fraternal organizations
* Athletic scholarships or programs other than community-sponsored programs for youth
* Courtesy advertising space
* Special events such as dinners, dances, or conventions that only indirectly benefit an organization
* Candidates for political office
* Partisan political organizations
* Individuals

Do's _____

- Summarize the policy upfront.
- Use the subject line to distinguish between a new or revised policy and an already established one. Without such a subject-line clue, the reader often skips reading the memo, thinking he is already informed about the stated policy.
- Mention the reasoning behind the policy or change in policy—unless this is obvious, as in the first memo. This explanation helps employees verify that they understand exactly what you are referring to.
- As much as possible, make policy sound like guidelines and benefits rather than restrictions and penalties.

- Give clear instructions for following the policy.
- Sprinkle lengthy policy statements with informative headings and use lists where possible. Rarely will an employee need to read the entire statement; he should be able to pinpoint immediately eligibility requirements, benefits, limitations, etc.

PROBLEMS, TO POINT OUT

Weak Model

Subject: Belton-Mason Rig--Jedd

The Jedd first came to my attention on October 6, 198-. Bob Seldon advised me that this was Universal's property. According to Bob, the specifications had been drawn up by Harrison Drilling Company and Scott Smith, who at that time worked for Universal but has since gone to work for Harrison Drilling. Bob also told me at that time that Universal and Harrison Drilling had an agreement whereby Universal paid for drilling tools at cost plus a 10 percent handling charge. We were to amortize this cost by adding $458 per day to the rig's daily rate.

After receiving this information, I instructed Accounting to debit Velasco Oil Tools and to credit expense account 406 for $169,994. We then decided to set up a rental rate in case this equipment happened to be used on a joint venture. (We did this by dividing the total cost by 90 days to arrive at a per-day rental.)

Later, the Jedd was used by the Northern Division. I asked Northern for a copy of Harrison Drilling's invoice and discovered that the daily rental had been charged to the Northern Division well. I then informed Accounting of our agreement, and they changed the first coding by way of voucher 208 to charge the total amount to account 501. I then asked that they send me a copy of each Harrison Drilling invoice for the Jedd so that I could keep track of when this equipment was paid for. As I received these invoice copies, I subtracted the chargeable amount from the total.

When I received a copy of the March billing, I noticed that the rig was moved onto GTR Blk #3 well #6, which is a joint venture. I then phoned Northern Division, advising them to charge the earlier-computed daily rental. They agreed that because this was Southern Division equipment, we should get the credit.

While visiting the Northern Division office during the last week of April, I inquired about the rental charge; they admitted that they didn't know how the equipment was being charged and raised some question about ownership of the Jedd. I told them, of course, that Universal did own it and that we had completely paid for it, plus 10 percent for handling. Upon further investigation, I found that the drilling contract had been renegotiated upward; Scott Smith at Harrison Drilling informed me that the daily rental charge had been removed when the contract was renegotiated.

A few days later, while talking to Scott Smith again, I was told that the equipment was theirs. Immediately I contacted Bob Seldon. Bob reviewed all the original correspondence and concluded that the wording was so vague that we'd probably have to go to court to determine ownership.

It appears that we need a decision about who owns the Jedd--especially since we've charged $327,000 rent to date. Also what do we do when the Jedd leaves our employ? Please advise what course of action I should take to clarify this problem.

Don'ts

- Don't use the once-upon-a-time format, giving details in chronological order. Such details have no meaning to the reader until she knows the problem—in this case, the disputed ownership of equipment.
- Don't dump the problem without offering options; at least suggest "next actions" to be investigated.

Good Models

Subject: Log Sheets for Graphics Terminal

Due to the increased use of the computer graphics equipment, we've had numerous scheduling conflicts that have resulted in some projects going beyond deadlines. I'd like to suggest a log sheet to reserve computer time.

We could schedule our time on the log sheet located in room T-989 by signing name, date, and estimated time requirements. If anyone must cancel this reservation, he or she should do so immediately to free the time slot for other work.

Time on the graphics equipment should be used only for final editing and graphing. Engineers will have to negotiate high-priority jobs among themselves. For work of lesser priority, we could use the terminals in C-445 and D-558.

Do you think this will work?

◆ ◆ ◆

Subject: Signature for Power of Attorney

I foresee a potential problem with our present policy with regard to proper acceptance of a signature under a power of attorney. According to law, the power-of-attorney procedure can be used by an absentee to conclude contractual obligations. Such procedure, however, always raises the possibility of fraud and could place us under a problem of collectibility on a loan under guarantee.

Therefore, I would suggest that we amend present company policy with regard to accepting signatures under power of attorney. I'd recommend that we handle all power-of-attorney signatures on a case-by-case basis at the vice-presidential level. This new policy should go into effect immediately.

Do's

- State the problem immediately.
- If they're not obvious, state all repercussions of the problem if a solution is not found.
- Suggest one or more possible solutions. At the very least, suggest steps to investigate possible options.
- Mention any deadline by which a solution must be found.
- Keep in mind that all details surrounding a problem are not necessarily relevant to its solution; be cautious about telling your reader more than he wants to know.

PROCEDURES

Good Models

Subject: Change in Procedure for Medical History and Physical
           Examination Records

We will no longer place employees' medical history and physical
examination forms in their personnel file. Rather, when these forms are
completed and returned to you, you should file them separately according
to the following procedure:
   a. Record employee's name on the physical examination form and
      medical history log sheet located in File Drawer C. Record in
      chronological order by the dates the completed forms are returned
      to you. (Note: Previously, we have filed these by date of exam
      shown on the form.)
   b. File the actual medical history or exam forms alphabetically by
      employee's last name in the expanding file in the records section,
      eighth floor.
   c. When an employee terminates, remove the employee's name from
      the chronological list in File Drawer C. Remove his or her medical
      history and exam form from the alphabetical expanding file and
      place it in his or her personnel folder filed in the inactive section,
      File Drawer D.

This change has been made so that departmental heads reviewing a file to
fill a vacancy will not permit an employee's medical history to influence
decisions on transfers or promotions.

◆ ◆ ◆

Subject: New Procedures for Reporting Flow-Computer Failures

Because of the 15 additional computers to be installed this year, verbal
reports of failures are no longer adequate to keep records up-to-date in our
headquarters office or to ensure proper maintenance. Therefore, we have
established the following procedures for reporting on failures. Use the
enclosed Flow Computer Inspection (FCI) form for developing this
information.

Please note that we have outlined the steps to be taken even before you
attempt to get the computer up and running and report the failure to
headquarters:

Steps to Get Computer Up and Running

(NOTE: If another employee is present, ask him or her to witness your inspection and cold start.)

1. Check CRT and note what is being displayed on the entire screen (Item 3 on the form).
2. If a request for programming is on the screen, note the date and time being displayed. Then record the <u>actual</u> date and time (Item 4 on the form).
3. If the screen is locked on any other display, note <u>which</u> display, along with the <u>date</u> and the <u>time</u> being displayed (Item 5 on the form).
4. Note whether the clock or computer is running (Item 6 on the form).
5. Go through a cold start. If the computer cannot be restarted at this time, check all voltages supplied to the cards (Item 8 on the form).
6. When the computer is running, complete the remainder of the information on the FCI form. If you cannot start the computer, call headquarters and wait for further instructions.

Steps for Making Verbal Report and Submitting
Flow-Computer Inspection Form

1. Call the clerk at extension 4489 to report the failure, being prepared to give the information you have recorded on the FCI form.
2. Record the failure on the log kept at your site.
3. Send the original FCI form and a printout at the time of the failure to Bob Duffy in Fort Worth. Make sure the printout contains a variable dump. This variable dump will help us to verify the constants being used in the volume calculation and possibly to locate past incorrect entries. Keep the pink copy for your records. Give the green copy to the inspection witness (if one was present at the time you attempted to restart the computer).

We have attached a sample completed form reporting the last failure at your site. If you have any questions about the reporting procedure or form, call us (ext. 4884).

◆ ◆ ◆

Subject: Documentation of Present Procedures for Purchase of All
Materials and Supplies

ORIGINATION OF
PURCHASE REQUEST

As materials and supplies are needed, prepare a purchase request by way of memo and submit it to the Purchasing Department. In your memo, give <u>all</u> the following information:

* Type and grade of material or supplies
* Quantity
* Technical specifications sheet, if necessary
* Date the material is needed
* Estimated cost
* Signature of approval by appropriate manager

PURCHASING
DEPARTMENT
PROCEDURES

Step	Action
1.	Purchasing logs in the request and assigns a buyer.
2.	Buyer checks the material request for corrections or other necessary information from the requester.
3.	Buyer requests and selects single or multiple bids as follows:
	a. When dollar value is less than $500, he will solicit only single bids, even on competitive materials.
	b. Bids for technical material will be predetermined by the material itself. If single source, he will solicit only one bid. If of a competitive nature, he will solicit multiple bids.
	c. If the material is technical, buyer transmits specification sheets to the bidder.
	d. Buyer reviews and analyzes all bids received, preparing and issuing a purchase order to the selected vendor.
4.	Clerks type all purchase orders placed by buyers and distribute copies to all appropriate parties (buyer, vendor, requester of materials).
5.	Clerks confirm to the requester by way of Form MS 200 the promised shipment date.
6.	Clerks file confirmations with the original purchase orders issued by the buyer.

Do's

• Give an overview of *what* the procedures cover, *whether this is a new or revised* procedure, *when* the procedure applies, *why* the procedural change, and *who* is involved. Any time you require employees to learn a new procedure, they want to know, "Why bother?" Also, when a reader understands the *why* behind procedures and *how* he fits into the big picture, he can make better judgments about exceptions or problems that develop. The actual steps of the procedure then will be the expanded "action" of the basic format.

• Use the subject line to show whether this is a new or a revised procedure or only documentation of present procedure.

• Give steps in chronological order.

• Begin at the beginning. Be careful regarding assumptions about the reader's knowledge. In fact, in most procedural writing, you should visualize yourself talking to the least-knowledgeable person who must follow your instructions.

• Identify each step that is a revision of existing procedure, explaining the purpose of the change.

• Highlight prominently any safety precautions or problems that may develop. If they are lengthy, promise specific details later in the chronological procedural step.

• Indicate each action in a separate sentence. Be particularly careful about linking phrases, items, and clauses with the word "and." Usually a more specific linking word is called for. For example: "Press the EV button and eject the tape." Is this one action or two? If you mean two separate actions, put them in separate sentences. If there is a time relationship, say, "Press the EV button. *Then* eject the tape." If there's a cause-and-effect relationship, say, "Press the EV button, thus ejecting the tape," or, "To eject the tape, press the EV button."

• Give illustrations or examples for complicated steps or explanations, as I just did in the above item.

• Acknowledge and note exceptions immediately after each step to which they apply.

• Prefer active-voice verbs. Because phrases telling who does what often sound awkward, writers are tempted to drop them out. But that's dangerous: Who does what is particularly important in procedures. Not: "Any emergency work orders should be brought to the attention of the maintenance supervisor for immediate action." But: "Each engineer should bring any emergency work order to the attention of the maintenance supervisor for immediate action." Or, "Bring any emergency work orders to the attention of the maintenance supervisor for immediate action." (The command form of the verb here indicates that the reader is the one who does the action.)

• Use headings, lists, or any creative design (see the previous memo) that will help the reader move quickly through the procedure to skim or relocate information.

PROGRESS REPORTS

Weak Model

Subject: January 198- Billings

Attached is a summary of our progress toward mailing the January billings. Our efforts have been slowed due to the following:
   a. We received billings three days later than usual due to computer downtime and program malfunction in statement printing.
   b. Some departments failed to submit equipment detail.
   c. Excess manual detailing was required due to ad valorem taxes.
   d. Christmas holidays and vacations interfered with the work schedule.

Don'ts

   • Don't be negative about your own efforts. Even if progress has been limited, as in this memo, state the progress in positive terms. (What percent of the billings has been mailed despite such great hindrances?) The memo focuses on reasons for failure rather than on progress.
   • Don't give problems or progress inhibitors without stating how you plan to overcome them. In this memo, after "b" there should be more explanation about how to get cooperation on future billings. After "c," the writer should have explained if manual detailing would be a recurring problem, and, if so, how to improve the situation.

Good Models

Subject: Progress Report--September 2 through September 14, 198-

Sale of Tall Oak Ranch
I have prepared and mailed a letter of intent as preliminary to the contract and am in the process of drafting a full contract. This contract should be ready for your signature October 1. A first draft is attached for your comments about payment schedule.

Payment on Atlanta Land Title Option and Loan
I have mailed the TFT check for $10,000 for option and TFTG check for $38,000 for the loan. The original executed documents and stock certificates have been filed permanently in Melvin Harris's office.

Purchase of San Pedro Plant
The deal is on hold, pending your decision on who is going to buy the plant. Warren doesn't want to spend the cash. Procedures prohibit Metcalf

from owning two plants in one county. Benjamin doesn't want to merge the two county plants he manages, because he's expecting to market one in the next six months. The owner is determined to close the deal as soon as possible and no later than December 15, 198-.

<u>New Claim Files Opened</u>
1. Claim of fraud--MC 303 ($33,000)
2. Limitation-boundary dispute--BD 4
3. Delinquent tax claim ($1,062)

I will advise you on these details as the claims progress. Please let me know your preference on the Tall Oak Ranch payment schedule and your decision about who will purchase the San Pedro plant.

◆ ◆ ◆

Subject: WNT Pilot Project Update

The WNT pilot project is now in the field-test stage.

Engineering reports that as of August 15, 198-, two tools are in service at the Los Angeles site. Although minor electronic problems have developed, the tools have run five jobs with good hyd-mechanical performance. One additional tool was shipped to Lafayette in July; however, the job was unsuccessful due to major electronics malfunctioning.

Engineering would like to do a few more tests on the tools before releasing them for production. The new target date for field-test sign-off is mid-October.

Revised charts are attached for your information.

Do's _____

● Summarize status or progress in one or two statements upfront, followed by next action, then details, then comments about attachments. If your progress report covers several projects, format each item individually—summary message, action, details, attachments. Note in the first memo, the "mini"-format under "Sale of Tall Oak Ranch."
● Be straightforward about problems.
● Show confidence rather than defeat by your tone. If you have problems, strain for the proverbial "light at the end of the tunnel."
● Use headings and lists in reporting on multiple items.
● If you must have approval or further information from the reader and have mentioned several separate items, you may close with a recap statement of the reader's total expected actions.

PROMOTIONS/RAISES, TO ANNOUNCE

Good Model

Subject: Promotion of Pam Myers to Senior Systems Analyst

We are pleased to announce that Pam Myers has been promoted to Senior Systems Analyst, effective October 1, 198-. Pam's first project will be designing and implementing the purchasing-control system.

As a graduate of the University of Arizona, Pam came to us as a computer programmer. She has since participated in all aspects of developing the security-control system, the capital-accounting projects, the vehicle-registration system, and finally the plant accounting year-end system.

With pride, we look forward to other contributions from Pam in her new role. Please join me in congratulating her.

Do's

- Announce the promotion or job-title change immediately.
- Briefly outline the new responsibilities so that others in the department will know how their tasks relate to those of the promoted employee.
- Briefly outline accomplishments and/or qualifications that led to the promotion.
- Show confidence and pride in the announcement, as if bestowing a reward for work well done. Your announcement may serve as motivation for other employees.

PROMOTIONS/RAISES, TO REQUEST

Weak Model

Subject: Request for Promotion to Administrative Assistant

I would like to request new responsibilities as Administrative Assistant. At the present time, my responsibilities involve providing secretarial support (typing, filing, and duplicating tasks) for 18 surveyors in the Technical Services Department. I have performed these monotonous duties for the past two years and would like the opportunity to move into something more challenging.

In the newly created position of Administrative Assistant, I would like to help with the following tasks:
* Assist in preparing the vice-presidential monthly summary
* Prepare the weekly job-status reports
* Make travel arrangements--including setting up a system to handle reservations, making cash advances, and filing expense reports
* Prepare time sheets and vacation schedules
* Distribute and follow up on FEC's
* Assist new employees in job orientation

Secretaries in both the Marketing and Accounting departments have assumed administrative-assistant positions and have improved their departments' efficiency; I am sure I can make equal contributions.

Additionally, transportation expenses have skyrocketed since I've moved across the city; unless something of this nature can be worked out, I will be forced to look elsewhere for opportunities for growth and a more appropriate salary.

Don'ts _____

• Don't ask for a raise/promotion because someone else received one. Such a request falls into the category of playing little red schoolhouse, where David asks teacher to give him a "B" because Jerry got a "B." Someone else may have received a promotion or raise because his work far exceeded yours; to be told such wouldn't be pleasant.

• Don't ask for a raise/promotion based on financial need. Because supervisors cannot very well verify true needs (even needs related to heavy medical expenses, etc.), they will often react against heartstring manipulation.

- Don't whine: "But I've been doing this same old job and everybody else gets the best projects." Or, "But you promised me last year that if I . . . so I am . . . so why don't you. . . ."
- Don't threaten with another offer unless you're sure the boss wants you to stay. Your threat of resignation may be the supervisor's easy way out of financial strain or may make way for another, more competent rising star. If you do have another offer or feel that you have no future with the present company, present your case as a "problem" about which you need your boss's advice: "I'd really like to stay because I enjoy what I do and appreciate our working relationship, but you know how hard it would be to turn down a $4,000 raise. . . ." You leave room for your boss to say either that he can meet the offer or that he can't meet the offer but can promise thus-and-so for the future. Then you can make your final decision with all the cards on the table.

Good Model

Subject: Accomplishments and Request for Additional Responsibilities

In the past two years my responsibility to provide secretarial support to 18 surveyors in the Technical Services Department has been a growth experience. In addition to performing the routine typing, filing, and duplicating tasks, I have had opportunities to contribute in significant ways to develop skills in other, related fields:

* Discovered improper expense reporting ($3,400 over a two-year period) for a surveyor who, upon management investigation, was terminated.
* Have gradually learned to handle routine inquiries from branch offices, saving surveyors many interruptions during the day. The average surveyor now must respond personally to fewer than three to five calls a week.
* Restructured the filing system and cut retrieval time for the average document from 10 minutes to less than a minute.
* Have become thoroughly acquainted with the expense-reporting and cash-advance system so that I now prepare such forms for six of the 18 surveyors.
* Organized a priority system for typing and filing required by the various surveyors; surveyors have commented on the system's fairness and effectiveness.

Therefore, in light of these contributions and newly acquired skills, I'd like to request a promotion to a newly created position of Administrative Assistant. This new position would allow my continued career growth and also relieve surveyors and Mack Albert of much routine paperwork that cuts into their more important assignments.

In this new role, I'd like to assist or be totally responsible in the following areas:
* Assist in preparing the vice-presidential monthly summary
* Prepare the weekly job-status reports
* Make travel arrangements--including setting up a system to handle reservations, making cash advances, and filing expense reports for all 18 surveyors
* Prepare time sheets and vacation schedules
* Distribute and follow up on FEC's
* Assist new employees in job orientation

I'd like to suggest a $3,000 raise as appropriate for such responsibilities. As mentioned during my last performance review, you recognize productivity and initiative; I would value such a promotion as evidence of your confidence in me on these points.

Of course, I'd be willing to train a replacement. In fact, I would like to suggest Cindy Hoffman (Marketing), who has worked with me temporarily during peak work loads. She has all the necessary typing, filing, and duplicating experience to handle those aspects of my present job.

Do I have your approval to assume these new duties--along with others you may want to add--thus increasing the effectiveness of our total department's operation?

Do's _____

● Begin with reasons and then follow with your request.
● Base your request on your own qualifications, accomplishments, assumed responsibilities, and goals. And always try to quantify past results—money saved, increased production, special contacts, or technical knowledge acquired. If you can't claim any such accomplishments, base your request on the very monotony of the job, its risks, or its significance to the company. For example: "The very monotony of this task makes money my only reward; therefore . . ."; or, "Due to chemical exposure, I feel that I cannot continue to risk health problems for my present salary. If the salary were higher, possibly I would reconsider . . ."; or "Since I'm the only engineer who has worked with similar designs and since this project will result in an approximate savings to the company of over $50,000 next year, I'd like to suggest a salary increase of. . . ."
● Find out and focus on the boss's standards for measurements: Volume of work? Creativity? Troubleshooting? Punctuality? Mentioning that you deserve a raise because you have accomplished something he doesn't consider valuable gets little attention.
● Emphasize the symbolic meaning of the promotion/raise rather than focusing on the money: "Such added responsibilities and appropriate salary

will, of course, allow me to feel as though I'm contributing significantly to the company's growth."

● If you have knowledge of the field and appropriate salary levels, name a specific raise amount. Be sure you request the highest figure in your range; often people "have not because they ask not." At least this amount establishes a point of negotiation.

● Suggest anyone you have groomed as a replacement. Or, if you have no one in mind, suggest that your job is in good shape to be handed over to someone else.

PROMOTIONS/RAISES, TO GRANT

Weak Model

Subject: Salary Increase

Effective June 1, 198-, your salary will increase to $1,833.33 per month or $22,000 annually. This rate represents a 9 percent increase over your current salary.

Don'ts

 • Don't sound begrudging or matter-of-fact. Remember that although employees will not be unhappy to receive a raise or promotion, they have other needs to be met, including the need for recognition and security. Unlike other "Approvals" mentioned in that category earlier in the book, granting raises and promotions calls for more elaboration. Even if the raise represents only a cost-of-living or grade-level increase, thank the employee for his contributions and try to compliment him on one specific area of achievement. End with a statement of goodwill that expresses wishes for a good future working relationship and/or more accomplishments.

Good Model

Subject: Approval to Assume Administrative Assistant Position

Sherrie,
With pleasure I'd like to approve your request to assume the position of Administrative Assistant, effective March, 1, 198-, with a salary increase of $2,000. You will continue to report to me.

After you settle into the job along the lines of those duties outlined in your memo, I'll be asking you to assume other tasks to help with routine correspondence from my office. I also think your suggestion that we contact Cindy Hoffman to assume the typing, filing, and duplicating tasks is a good one and will ask that as your first duty you contact Cindy about her interests. In the event she is unavailable or uninterested in the move, please arrange to contact Personnel for their recommendations in hiring a replacement.

Thanks for reminding me what significant contributions you have made to the department during the past two years. I do particularly value your initiative in restructuring the filing system and also your willingness to relieve the surveyors of the "routine" matters as you have had the time. As I mentioned in your last performance appraisal, you are the kind of dependable employee we'd like to keep.

Do's

- Give your approval immediately. Clarify the effective date, salary agreement, and to whom the employee will report—if a change is necessary.
- Make clear any trial period with the new responsibilities, mentioning date and review standards for the permanent assignment. (In the above memo, there was no trial period mentioned in the administrative assistant promotion.)
- Approve with elaboration and with commendation for a job well done, specifically mentioning one or two of the most important contributions or skills acquired. But remember that effusive flattery sounds insincere.
- Show confidence and pride, rather than obligation, in granting approval; bestow the promotion and/or raise as if it were a reward—which it is.

PROMOTIONS/RAISES, TO DECLINE

Good Model

Subject: Administrative Assistant Position

Thank you for reminding me what significant contributions you have made to the department during the past two years. I do particularly value your initiative in restructuring our filing system and also your willingness to relieve the surveyors of the "routine" matters as you have had time. As I mentioned in your last performance appraisal, you are the kind of dependable employee we'd like to keep.

As you know, however, we have not hired any new employees in the past three months due to economic conditions in the industry as a whole. Likewise, money budgeted for raises has been frozen until we see some turnaround in contract sales. But in light of your present skills and duties, I'd like to change your job title to Administrative Assistant, without all the additional duties outlined in your memo, and, I'm sorry to say, without a raise at this time. Even though your assuming such tasks would relieve surveyors of routine paperwork, I'm afraid that with such a sluggish economy their increased time would not necessarily lead to increased business.

Please do know, however, that I have noted your accomplishments and plan to give these added responsibilities and commensurate raise further attention. Perhaps when business picks up so that we hire an additional three surveyors, we can then assign you additional duties and hire extra secretarial help as you outlined.

Do's

● Begin on a positive note; thank the employee for his accomplishments, initiative, new idea, or at least interest in assuming new responsibilities.

● Give adequate reasons for declining a raise or promotion. If the employee is deficient in some areas, point them out in a positive way and tell him specifically how he can improve and what your standards of measurement are. If "no money" is the claim, be convincing. Be careful with this reason, however, so that you don't start financial-problem rumors that may create panic among the ranks. If you have no freedom to grant raises because salaries follow preexisting guidelines, explain that.

● Offer substitutes when you can. In the model above, the supervisor offers to change the title, something that costs him nothing and meets a need for prestige and recognition of achievement.

● State under what conditions you may change your mind about the decision. Promise later review or state circumstances that may alter the present situation. If, on the other hand, you would like to see the employee leave, tactfully wish him success in "finding something that may give you the opportunities you deserve."

● Express appreciation for the employee's strengths.

PROPOSALS

Weak Model

Subject: Proposal for Security Guard Service at Bayar Terminal

Good contract service companies meet the needs of their customers, whatever those needs might be. In our case, that means control of the flow of personnel, vehicles, and materials/products entering and departing the Bayar Terminal. Weekly, this coverage would amount to 120 hours straight-time, eight hours overtime, and a supervisor's salary. Somewhere down the line, we should also investigate emergency support in cases of strike.

I have investigated three security contract services: Bilton, Security Unlimited, and Guardsmen. I identified these three by interviewing six company security offices in this area--none of whom gave strong recommendations for any particular company. I should also mention that over half gave unsolicited and unfavorable comments about two other companies—Pewton and Fairfax. Therefore, I did not bother to check out these.

Bilton

Bilton will agree to give our Bayar representative final approval on guards assigned here. The company has no specific criteria that calls for its guards to have past military/civilian police experience. Although I told their representative that it would be helpful in Bayar operations if guards had good verbal skills, the representative could not guarantee writing skills. However, all guards do speak English; how well, of course, is always debatable. The company does run reference checks and requires physical exams but does not require its personnel to take polygraphs. Bilton is a local company and could provide close supervision. Such supervisory visits are irregularly scheduled, and the representative I spoke with could not guarantee how frequently these visits occur. As far as compensation goes, hourly wages are comparable to our entry-level positions; but the company would not provide details of its benefit package, i.e., holiday and overtime compensation, vacations, and insurance. However, I suppose these to be adequate to attract permanent employees. Bilton does provide eight hours of training prior to guard assignment to a duty station and minimal first-day supervision on the job. Cost for 24-hour service would be approximately $58,500 per year.

Security Unlimited

Security Unlimited will agree to final approval of all personnel by our Bayar representative. However, I don't know how much good that approval would be, because the company will not furnish copies of reference checks. I would estimate that 50 percent of all applicants could be ruled out with such checks. In fact, a guard service in town has recently been identified as the employer of a prime murder suspect in a case involving a previous employer. However, the employees do take a polygraph and physical exam; we would have access to these results. Security Unlimited does guarantee weekly supervisory visits, provides six hours of training prior to guard assignment, but does not provide personal on-the-job supervision. However, the representative assured me that all questions arising on site can be taken care of by phone or special requested visits. The compensation is far below our scale for entry-level positions; neither would the company provide details about its benefit package. Being a local company also, Security Unlimited would provide service for $63,385 per year.

Guardsmen

Guardsmen will agree to final approval of all personnel by our Bayar representative. The company rep seemed very cordial in offering to provide reference checks, polygraph exam results, and physical exam results. However, the applicants are not required to have either military or civilian police experience. Nor could the rep guarantee written fluency of the guards, although all must have good oral communication skills. Like the other two companies, Guardsmen is local and can provide close supervision and backup personnel for emergency support. Supervisors make weekly visits to all guard sites. Training includes 12 hours of prior instruction in legal authority, search/seizure, personal appearance and conduct, emergency plans, and safety. Training also includes personal supervision for the first two days on the job. Beginning salaries are comparable to ours, with increases based on merit. Guardsmen will provide our required services for $75,750 per year.

Security services are like football tickets. If you want to sit on the 50-yard line, you must pay a fair price. However, if you can be satisfied with seats in the end zone, they come a little cheaper.

Don'ts

- Don't include all the details of your investigation or alternatives without drawing conclusions and making recommendations. Such is merely "legwork" and not to be confused with an effective proposal.
- Don't grab the first arrangement that comes to mind. In this case, the writer has chosen a company-by-company format. Notice how hard his reasoning and details are to follow, interpret, and remember. Also, the danger is great in such an arrangement that a detail or two will be omitted, resulting in an apples-to-oranges final comparison.
- Don't mix pros and cons. If you do choose to arrange by company, service, or product category, at least separate the pros from the cons, the benefits from the disadvantages, the acceptable from the unacceptable.

- Don't assume your reader knows the criteria for weighing details. In the above memo, you must read almost the complete proposal before you learn what the writer expects of the security service with regard to personnel hiring and approval practices, salary and benefits, training, skills, supervision, and location.
- Don't get bogged down telling the reader about your trouble gathering information. For the most part, she cares only about your results and conclusions. Notice the unnecessary information in the second paragraph of the memo.
- Don't equate the quality of your proposal with the length of the recommendation or the money involved; there's no correlation.

Good Models

Subject: Proposal for Security Guard Service at Bayar Terminal

Due to our growing needs for security at the Bayar Terminal (198- estimated loss from stolen goods amount to $200,000), I recommend that we engage a contract security service to control the flow of personnel, vehicles, and materials/products entering and departing from our terminal. After interviewing six company security offices in the area, I narrowed my investigation to three security services: Bilton, Guardsmen, and Security Unlimited. I propose that we offer a contract to Guardsmen at an annual cost of $75,750.

Guardsmen will allow our final approval on assigned guards and will provide results of all reference checks, physical exams, and polygraph tests. Their representative has also allowed access to salary schedules and benefits packages, those being equal to ours at entry-level positions. The guards receive 12 hours of instruction and two days' personal supervision on the job. As a local company, Guardsmen schedules weekly unannounced supervisory visits and can be flexible in providing backup support.

If you accept this proposal, I'd suggest implementation be turned over to Darrell Bennaham with January 1 as our target date.

This recommendation is based on the following criteria and investigative information from Bilton, Security Unlimited, and Guardsmen.

Hiring Practices
The security company should be willing to go into detail about how guards are selected; all guards should be subject to final approval by our Bayar representative. The security company should provide results of all reference checks, polygraph exams, and physical exams. Also, guards

should have acceptable oral and written communication skills. Previous experience as a military/civilian policeman would also be advantageous.
* Bilton does not require their personnel to take polygraphs.
* Security Unlimited will not agree to furnish reference checks. This would suggest that background checks are not always made, and such checks would, in my estimation, eliminate approximately 50 percent of all applicants.
* Guardsmen meets all our hiring criteria except as noted in the next sentence.
* None of the companies could guarantee that its guards had previous military/civilian police experience or acceptable writing skills.

Supervision

Bayar should require regular weekly visits by an area supervisor. Without this backup supervision, Bayar Terminal personnel will find themselves repeatedly involved in details of security management, supposedly provided by the security company itself.
* Bilton's procedures call for only "unspecified" visits by its supervisors and would not state how often these visits occur.
* Security Unlimited guarantees weekly unannounced supervisory visits.
* Guardsmen guarantees weekly unannounced supervisory visits.

Compensation

Hourly rates should be comparable to those paid terminal personnel at entry-level positions, with scheduled increases based on merit. The company's benefits package should also include uniforms and personal equipment, holiday and overtime compensation, vacations, hospitalization, and life insurance. Such compensation suggests permanence and more highly skilled workers.
* Neither Bilton nor Security Unlimited would provide the details of its benefits package, both merely saying it was "adequate."
* Security Unlimited's beginning wage is far below that of our entry-level employees.
* Guardsmen has provided all this requested information. Beginning salaries are comparable to those of our personnel, and raises are based on merit.

Training

Since no state certification is required, the company should provide training prior to posting personnel at the terminal. Guard training should include legal authority, search/seizure, personal appearance and conduct, emergency plans, and safety. New personnel should work under personal supervision for at least 24 hours before assuming duties alone.
* Bilton provides eight hours of training prior to assigning a guard to a permanent duty station, and minimal first-day personal supervision.

* Security Unlimited provides six hours of training, but no personal on-the-job supervision.
* Guardsmen provides 12 hours' training and two days' personal on-the-job supervision.

Location
Companies should be located within 50 miles of our terminal to allow for close and frequent supervision and flexibility in providing backup personnel.

* All three companies are local.

Costs
Our requirements for sufficient security include one supervisor/instructor and three security officers (one officer to cover the three eight-hour shifts). Weekly, this should amount to 120 hours of straight time, eight hours of overtime, and the supervisor's salary. Costs for the security service, of course, vary in line with how well the companies meet the above criteria:

* Bilton--$58,500
* Security Unlimited--$63,385
* Guardsmen--$75,750

Security services are like football tickets. If you want to sit on the 50-yard line, you must pay a fair price. However, if you can be satisfied with seats in the end zone, they come a little cheaper.

◆ ◆ ◆

Subject: Supervisory Skills Training Program Proposal

Employee Development has been conducting an in-house supervisory course that focuses primarily on theory and information about management concepts and company policies. We would like to propose additional training for first- and second-line supervisors, focusing on skills only-- specific behavioral guidance in supervising and motivating employees to increase productivity.

The program would be administered with the help of TAG Consulting, Inc., a Phoenix firm. The total cost of $52,000 will cover customized behavior models, videotaped introductory and practice sessions, six line managers and/or staff certified by TAG as qualified trainers, two classes (20 participants each) of trained supervisors, and trainer manual and participant workbook for reproduction.

Program Objectives
Research shows that attempts to change attitudes of supervisors by logical presentation of theory rarely succeed. Therefore, this program focuses on changing on-the-job behavior. The training will focus on skills such as active listening, self-esteem, reinforcement techniques, goal-setting, and

other concerns identified by a needs-analysis questionnaire administered to
our supervisors.

The actual design will involve videotaping company supervisors as they
effectively model the desired behavioral skills. These tapes will provide
positive models to use in later training sessions. Supervisors will then
practice the specific behaviors demonstrated by the videotape models until
they gain confidence in their ability to handle the same situations on the
job. Both participants and trainers provide critiques during the practice
sessions. Follow-up sessions will allow "report back" time in which
participants report on success, problems, and questions arising from
on-the-job application.

A schedule of actual consultant-led meetings for needs analysis, program
design, and videoscripting and -taping is attached. Also, I've attached a
sample format for a "typical" session, along with probable topics for all
sessions.

Cost Breakdown

Production costs	$20,000
Actual training costs	18,500
Travel and miscellaneous	
consultant expenses	8,200
Written materials	5,300
	$52,000

Of this fee, $20,000 (production costs payable after videoscripting) will
come out of our 198- budget allocations for equipment. The remaining
$32,000 (payable as training expenses occur) will come from the 198-
budget.

Research on Effectiveness and Acceptance of Program

Research has been extensive, involving 18 firms and their accompanying
methodology, client references, and TAG's self-reported results. After
narrowing the programs down to three for careful examination, we
observed various phases of the TAG program as it was being implemented
in other companies (Howell, Inc.; Allied; and Cascade Corporation) and
made our selection on TAG's own records and their clients' records of
success.

Further, we have verbally presented the program to key executives in our
own company to ask for their insight on possible problems of
implementation and about their willingness to help with the planning and
scripting. A. B. White, C. T. Smith, R. J. Young, and V. B. Brown all
enthusiastically support the program and have given us suggestions for
scheduling participants from their particular divisions. D. E. Chung has
expressed concern that supervisors may be unwilling to be videotaped in

practice sessions; however, we feel that his concerns will not materialize with the skillful handling of TAG consultants.

Finally, of course, our prime impetus has come from participants in past in-house supervisory courses. Their repeated comments have been that they need "something practical to really use back on the job." These concerns from supervisors again surfaced on the 198- needs-analysis survey conducted in February.

Confidently, we suggest that this supervisory-skills program will produce the results that our personnel have requested. Immediate approval of this proposal will enable us to use the start-up money from our 198- money and schedule our first TAG planning consultation in December.

Do's

- Give the overall scope of the proposal, specific recommendation, and total cost upfront.
- Choose the detail arrangement most appropriate for your particular subject. Generally, that means stating criteria, features, or options first. Then show how each product, machine, service, person, or company meets the criteria you've established. Such an arrangement lets your reader "keep score" more easily and also ensures more equal comparisons than otherwise. You may find, however, any number of other suitable arrangements—geographical, costliness, advantages vs. disadvantages. Whatever arrangement you choose, move from most to least significant points and do not mix pros and cons in any category.
- Weigh and interpret facts and details. Is a specific detail beneficial? Harmful? To be expected? Indicative of a trend? Competitive? Questionable? Why? For example, in the first memo, the writer tells us that results on reference checks is a must. Also, adequate salary and benefits packages suggest that guards would be more permanent and have better skills. Don't simply state a fact and expect your reader to decide if that fact is desirable or undesirable, important or unimportant, acceptable or unacceptable.
- When possible, break down total cost so that the reader can "play" with the figures, omitting or increasing specific options to fit any budget limitations. Note the breakdown in the training proposal.
- Add authority. Can you gather more facts? Interview experts or clients? Survey staff preferences and needs? Give case studies? Produce figures from past years or from other companies?
- Identify subjective statements as such. Add clarifying comments such as "in my opinion," "according to experts in the field," "this fact suggests," or "due to claims of past clients."
- Suggest how the proposal be implemented. Mention individuals or departments to handle specifics, and, if appropriate, suggest a target date for implementation.

RECORDS, TO CHECK AND CORRECT

Good Models

Subject: Continuing Costs on K10743 Madra Isle Block 266

Today Fred Brownstone, owner of a 10 percent working interest in the above Madra Isle property, phoned to request an explanation of why he is still being billed for costs attributable to this property. Work was abandoned in March 198-.

Would you please contact Mr. Brownstone (P.O. Box 2588, Pine Bluff, Arkansas) to explain why costs are continuing to come in at this late date and copy us with your memo?

According to our records, all of the following billings have been paid except those for April and October:

April	$211.79
May	337.33
June	58.99
July	699.35
August	473.88
September	88.98
October	68.24

◆ ◆ ◆

Subject: Duplication of Exchange Numbers 7793

Plant Revenue has notified me that we have a duplication of exchange numbers--Bellasco 7793 and Warner 7793.

I'd suggest that we cancel Warner 7793, since it has been inactive since May 198-. Or, if you prefer, we can assign Bellasco 7793 another number?

Please verify the duplication and then advise both us and Plant Revenue about correcting our records as soon as possible. Major billings are due to go out to Bellasco within the week.

◆ ◆ ◆

Subject: Tank-Car Shipments Held--Invoicing

Please review the attached list of tank-car shipments to Myrtle Springs, Louisiana, that were held an excessive length of time from February 6–9; advise me of any discrepancies.

If I have not heard from you within 15 days of this memo date, I will assume that you agree, and I will issue an invoice to cover the shipments.

Do's

• State immediately that you want to verify, question, or correct such-and-such record.
• Give full details about the records to which you refer, not simply the one item you need to check. With only one identifying detail, the reader may have trouble locating the information or may overlook other discrepancies that neither of you knows about.
• Ask for a response so that you know your message was received and your requested action taken. If your verification is routine, you may use the "unless I hear from you . . ." approach. Caution: What happens if your intended reader is out of the office for two weeks?
• Unless it is obvious to your reader, mention the importance of a speedy correction. If you have in mind a certain response date, say so.
• Assume a tone of mutual responsibility and competence. Never imply that your records could contain no error and that the reader's records are always the incorrect ones. (Avoid: "Our records show that . . . ; would you please correct yours accordingly.") Rarely is it necessary to place blame for the error; rather focus on verifications and/or corrections.

REFERENCES, TO REQUEST

Good Model

Subject: Reference Request for Sales Rep Transfer

As I mentioned to you during our phone conversation last month, I have had my eye open for a sales job for some time. At last, I have had the opportunity to interview with Martin Waggoner for such an opening in the Western Division and have given your name as a reference.

Should he contact you about previous work under your supervision (February 198- to June 198-), I'd appreciate any comments you can make about my interpersonal skills in dealing with customers there in the office and about my product knowledge gained in relaying such information from headquarters to field personnel. The sales rep job, of course, heavily depends on skills in these areas, as well as initiative and organizational ability in handling a larger territory.

Thanks so much for any help you can give in arranging this transfer.

Do's

● Mention the dates you worked under the reader's supervision, particularly if there has been an interlude elsewhere.
● Give the reader specific information about the job for which you're applying. This will enable her to highlight the abilities and traits most appropriate for the prospective assignment.
● Help the reader think; remind her of duties performed that would prepare you for the desired job.
● Thank the reader for her efforts. Remember that this request, often considered a personal rather than a business matter, takes time away from other (to your reader) more important tasks.

(NOTE: If you are requesting a reference for someone you're considering hiring, the same guidelines apply. If you want specific answers, ask specific questions. Explain what the job entails so that the reader can comment on specific skills and characteristics necessary for the outlined responsibilities. Otherwise, you'll likely get the routine reference that basically says, "John is a good old boy.")

REFERENCES, TO SUPPLY

Good Models

Subject: Reference for Henry Malone

Yes, I'd be happy to recommend Henry Malone as a member of your legal staff there in Chicago. He has worked with me since June 198- and has provided legal opinions on just about every governmental regulation we've encountered. He's self-motivated, thorough in his research, and knowledgeable in all aspects. Although not particularly articulate, Henry does communicate effectively in writing. I only wish there was a way to give him the promotion here that he deserves; I hate to lose him.

I wish both of you the best when his transfer is approved.

◆   ◆   ◆

Subject: Reference for John Guerierre

Bill,

John did speak to me earlier about moving into your department as soon as there was an opening.

While working for me since July 198-, John has demonstrated considerable ability in all our statistical functions; he is organized and meticulous with details. Seldom do I find a mistake in his work.

He has had a problem, however, with tardiness. My records show that he has been tardy 30 percent of the time, and for our department this creates a work-flow problem. Perhaps we run a tighter ship here than most departments do, and this lateness may not be a significant problem in your area. Also, let me add that John has gone through a recent divorce that may have had some effect on his initiative to get to work on time. In a new environment with new responsibilities, perhaps he would be more conscientious about punctuality.

If you have other specific questions, please phone.

Do's

- Include the facts of the employee's work—major responsibilities and dates under your supervision.
- Include both strengths and weaknesses in job performance.

● Comment on personal characteristics that make the individual a good employee.

● Keep in mind legal safeguards: Be honest; make sure you have proof of what you say; bear no malice. If you cannot give a strong recommendation, perhaps you can defer to someone "who can give a stronger recommendation that I can." But don't let personal feelings affect your evaluation of a person's abilities; keep in mind that people react differently to various supervisory approaches. Remember that often the employee transferring to another department may see your comments.

● Verify the reason for the employee's leaving your department.

● Be brief.

REMINDERS

Weak Model

Subject: Career Open House

In light of last year's misunderstanding, this is to remind you that the Career Open House is an effort to recruit professionals from college campuses, not an open house for our present employees.

Don'ts _____

- Don't "take up where the last conversation (or memo) left off," so to speak. This example sounds like an afterthought and will likely raise more questions than it answers: What Career Open House? When is it scheduled? Can we invite any college seniors we know? Is there some sort of career development presentation that we as employees *can* attend? Why not?

Good Models

Subject: Career Open House Reminder

This memo comes to remind you of the Career Open House scheduled for April 2 in the main lobby reception area of the first-floor plaza. Company representatives will be on hand to talk with visiting college seniors and answer their questions about career possibilities with Gilbert Gas. If you know of college seniors interested in our company, please feel free to invite them.

Although this event is not open to present employees, a similar presentation to meet your career development needs will be scheduled later in the summer.

◆ ◆ ◆

Subject: Reminder for Toastmaster's Meeting

Remember that the Toastmaster's Club will meet Tuesday, October 14, at 11:45 a.m. in the Oak Room rather than the usual Teak Room at the Marietta Club.

Please call Karen Harris (ext. 225) by Monday, October 13, to make lunch reservations.

As we decided last week, we will be discussing a new meeting day and publicity ideas for extended company involvement.

Do's

- State upfront the item you wish to remind the reader about and his expected action.
- Make the reminder as complete as the first announcement. Repeat all necessary information—time, date, place, purpose, topics of concern, deadlines, etc. If the reminder changes a reader's mind about the event or the action, he shouldn't have to go elsewhere in the files to get information to reverse his decision or carry out the action.
- Mention in both the subject line and body of the memo the word "reminder." Otherwise, the reader may think you are sending him new information containing some detail about which he was unaware beforehand.
- If the reminder is sent due to some change in the former plan or announcement, call special attention to that change. To add emphasis, place that detail alone in a separate paragraph or underline it.

REORGANIZATIONS

Good Model

Subject: Companywide Reorganization

The reorganization of the Research/Development and Marketing divisions represents a fundamental change in Universal's management approach--both philosophically and structurally. Underlying the restructuring is the belief that Universal must become more aggressive in exploiting growth opportunities overseas. Toward that objective, planning and execution of those plans require central leadership to coordinate worldwide entrepreneurial management.

Under our present reorganization the Research/Development and Marketing divisions will serve as international resources for assistance and coordination, as well as provide effective communication among all our locations. Primarily, this strengthened matrix will help us focus on specific goals and fix accountability for achievement.

With this direction, we will devote financial resources only to those projects that best satisfy our worldwide, long- and short-range objectives for profitability.

To give you a better idea of who does what, the attached Summary Table of Organization briefly outlines responsibilities of new positions and divisions. These organizational changes should improve control of product introduction and marketing effort.

With pleasure I'd like to announce the following key appointments and promotions:
    Juan Guiterrez--Director of Marketing
    Harvey Mahon--Director of Research/Development
    Myrtle Ivy--General Manager, Australia
    Kelly Little--General Manager, Japan
    Morton Tinsley--General Manager, England
Shortly, you will receive communication from these individuals about help and direction they can furnish you on specific projects.

With all confidence of extended growth and greater personal achievement from each of you, I look forward to our May meeting in Houston.

Do's

- Inform readers of the primary focus of the reorganizational effort. Highlight specific divisions, departments, or positions created or eliminated. Of course, with this subject, the message and the action become one.

- Explain any follow-up action that may be expected from your reader or any action from higher-ups that will affect your reader.

- Give the "why" or theory behind the restructuring. That information gives all employees a foundational basis for rethinking their own objectives and makes later directives from new supervisors more understandable and authoritative.

- Include a diagram, chart, or summary to help employees visualize the restructured chain of command. Be sure this visual aid explains how the newly organized positions, divisions, or departments relate to all employees on your distribution list.

- Be tactful if the reorganization is to correct an existing personnel problem and/or eliminate positions.

REPRIMANDS

Weak Model

Subject: Interfering with Assigned Work

Would you please tell me what emergency at Bloomington's was so urgent that you pulled one of our men (Jack Donne) to be a "gofer" without getting his supervisor's approval?

Don'ts _____

- Don't hide a reprimand behind a trapping question. If the reader has committed an offense, say so. If you mean only to verify what you have been told or have assumed, ask for verification outright.
- Don't leave to the reader's discretion how you want the action, behavior, attitude, or situation corrected.

Good Models

Subject: Supervisory Approval on Change in Assigned Work

In the future, please be sure to get a supervisor's approval before changing anyone's job assignment.

Yesterday Jack Donne was sent without his supervisor's approval to Bloomington's on what I consider a routine, rather than emergency, errand. Such a situation undercuts authority and may create serious problems with the abandoned project assignment.

◆ ◆ ◆

Subject: Improper Safety Glasses

Metal-frame glasses are unacceptable for safety protection in our production area. I noticed that you were not wearing the proper safety glasses yesterday, July 7, 198-, and I checked with Marvin Kincaide about the violation. He informed me that on June 28 you were given a prescription form and a pair of goggles to wear over your metal frames until you received the proper safety glasses.

Please get the safety glasses within the next two weeks; until then, I ask that you wear the goggles issued to you.

This safety rule is for your own protection. If you are having a problem in getting the prescription filled, please let me know.

◆   ◆   ◆

Subject: Sick-Leave Restriction

This is to notify you that effective January 1, 198-, you must submit medical certification to support all absences due to illness. This restriction will remain in effect for at least six months and until further notice from me.

If your substantiated absences, medical or otherwise, exceed three days during this next six-month period, we will be forced to terminate your employment.

You are being placed under this restriction because an analysis of your attendance record indicates that some of your absences may have been unjustified. Your records show that you missed work on three Mondays and four Fridays during the last quarter: October 3, 14, 17, 24; November 4, 18; and December 2.

Do's

- Focus on the offense. Communicate clearly and specifically what behavior, attitude, or decision is in error and how you expect it to be corrected.
- Document your complaints and past reprimands.
- Impress upon the reader the importance for corrective action and get him to "buy into" complying with your request or company policy.
- When possible and not already obvious, explain why the behavior, situation, or decision needs correction or why the policy or rule has been established. A *why* generally improves cooperation.
- On second or later reprimands, warn the reader of next action if the problem is not corrected.
- Try to minimize resentment by focusing on behavior and results or consequences rather than motives or intentions.
- Match your tone to the seriousness and frequency of the offense, getting firmer after a first warning: "I noted there's a problem in that you . . ." to, "This is the second warning about . . . " to, "I must warn you that any repetition of this situation will be cause for immediate dismissal."

RESIGNATIONS

Good Models

Subject: Resignation

I offer my resignation as Buyer of Materials and Services, effective April 6, 198-.

♦ ♦ ♦

Subject: Resignation

Please accept my resignation as Associate Chemist at Neuhauser Research, Inc.; my last day will be August 15, 198-.

While enjoying assigned projects and contributing to the company's overall growth, I feel that my work tasks here have not allowed me to investigate projects in which I developed a keen interest during my graduate studies. Therefore, I have accepted a position more in line with those interests at Meadows Chemical Company.

This decision has been difficult due to the rewarding relationships developed during the past three years. Please accept my thanks for your unquestionable support and leadership here at Neuhauser.

Do's _____

● Give your job title, resignation, and effective date. If you're leaving under unpleasant circumstances, this one statement is all you need.

(If you are leaving willingly and/or under pleasant circumstances, you may wish to follow these remaining guidelines.)

● Give your reason for leaving. Be careful, however, that you do not include anything that may come back to haunt you on later reference checks: "I feel that I have not been able to contribute significantly here because . . ."; ". . . your unwillingness to accept my new ideas about . . ."; ". . . because of the continuing conflict between Tom Storres and me." If you mention your reason, make it acceptable to a future employer: ". . . limited opportunities for advancement"; ". . . want to assume another position more in line with my training and career objectives . . ."; ". . . would like to move back to the Midwest to be nearer my children." If you do take a stab at your employer, at least let the memo "cool off" a few days to make sure you are willing to bear the repercussions.

- State future plans.
- Express gratitude for past experiences and relationships.
- Be brief.
- Be sincere. Omit whatever items above that you can't express truth-fully.

RESPONSIBILITIES, NEW, TO REQUEST

Good Model

Subject: Coordination of Oral Presentation Efforts

In the past couple of years, our combined staff has made approximately 200 presentations either to upper management or to clients and prospective clients. But needless to say, our track record in assembling the materials and information for the presentations leaves room for improvement.

Our engineers, graphics staff, technical editors, and librarian all testify to the harried, last-minute rush that befalls us on many projects--projects on which we usually have several weeks' advance notice. In fact, in two recent situations (McBride Corporation and Huffdale, Inc.), hastily prepared presentations contributed to a loss of $140,000 in potential contracts.

To solve this problem, I suggest that we designate a Presentation Coordinator to unify efforts in assembling and preparing materials and gathering information. If this idea seems feasible to you, I'd be willing to take on this additional duty.

Briefly, let me outline the coordination methods I have in mind:
* Engineers would set up an initial appointment with the coordinator to discuss specific topic and needs. The coordinator could suggest other information and audiovisuals on hand in the company library.
* The coordinator would work with the technical editor and graphics staff to oversee the production of materials requested by the engineers.
* The coordinator would arrange to schedule photography on a priority basis.
* The coordinator would maintain logs for reserving audiovisual equipment for each presentation.
* The coordinator would work with Maintenance to ensure that all equipment for presentation is in good working order.
* The coordinator would "run errands" as necessary to free individual secretaries for typing final drafts and handouts.
* The coordinator would arrange for delivery of all materials and necessary equipment to the presentation site.

All the coordinator's activities, of course, would be subject to each engineer's specific direction and approval.

I'd suggest that we announce the Presentation Coordinator's function to the engineers and try the system on a voluntary basis for two months. I have already mentioned this idea to three of our senior engineers (Hastings, Green, Lambert), and they seem willing to give the plan a try.

After two months, we could reevaluate the idea's effectiveness. A committee of engineers then could make a final recommendation to you whether to continue the coordinator's function, with all engineers required to avail themselves of the service.

I'm eager to contribute to our efforts in delivering our services more effectively. What do you think?

Do's

- State the new responsibilities in the form of a problem to be solved. Discover how some situation, event, or requirement inhibits smooth operation, and then develop a solution.
- Start by elaborating on the "problem" (although your main message is that you want to assume new responsibilities) and its significance in time, money, and/or operation. Your recommended action, then, will be your request for more responsibility to solve the problem. The details will include how you will carry out the new responsibilities to attack the problem.
- Offer built-in checks by suggesting review or feedback at specific stages of your plans.
- Demonstrate that you agree with your supervisor's goals.
- Be authoritative about your solutions and new responsibilities. Make sure they are well thought out and that others perceive the situation the same as you do.
- Show willingness to share the credit for the results of your idea.

RESPONSIBILITIES, NEW, TO DELEGATE

Good Model

Subject: Approval of New Responsibilities as Presentation Coordinator

Your idea of designating a Presentation Coordinator seems promising. I'll announce these new responsibilities for your position as coordinator with a memo to the entire division later in the week.

I do, however, want to modify your outlined plan; I prefer to make this a unified, nonvoluntary effort from the very beginning. This will allow us to measure the full effectiveness of coordination without having problems from those engineers who continue "to do their own thing" about using the equipment and duplicating visuals and information already available.

Your new responsibilities will entail commensurate authority to schedule use of all audiovisual equipment and materials and to approve related expenses. Such expenses, as always, you will charge back to each budgeted project. Because your duties will be a service to the engineering staff, you will, of course, need to check with them for final approval of projected costs.

I'd suggest that after you coordinate the first few presentations you report back to me about successes and problems. I'll be glad to work with you in getting this much-needed service off the ground.

Do's _____

• Grant the new responsibilities immediately. Remember that when you say "yes," you can omit the reasons. If you are declining to approve the responsibilities, see " 'No' Replies," page 121.

• Give adequate instruction for delegated responsibilities. Anticipate special problems and make sure the tasks are well outlined.

• Grant the necessary authority to accompany responsibility. In the previous memo, that means the total authority to schedule equipment use and to authorize expenses within the limits established by the project engineer.

• Do suggest "feedback" steps and offer help. Assure the reader that you do not expect instant success and that you welcome the chance to help him overcome obstacles. Otherwise, you may not get any "bad news" until the situation has become hopeless.

RUMORS

Weak Model

Subject: Percaarisus Permentol

After hearing several conversations at the convention last week, I became increasingly aware that some of you are trying to kill this product line before it ever catches hold. A negative attitude on your part will kill the promotion quicker than a defective product anytime.

This is an excellent product line, and we intend to get sales off dead center. Concentrated effort will mean some additional time in zeroing in on primary markets; but once you qualify your leads, you will begin to pick up additional customers and enjoy substantial commissions. If you need help in qualifying specific leads, contact Frank Bohon.

I want these rumors about product test results to cease, and I expect to see sales of this line on your next reports.

Don'ts _____

- ● Don't feel that you must trace the origin of a rumor or place blame for its spreading.
- ● Don't use an accusatory, watchdog tone when you intend to mend rumor damage; such a tone tends to cast a shadow on the truth or at least fuel further speculation.

Good Model

Subject: Percaarisus Permentol--Marketing Efforts

At the convention last week I heard some of you express concern over the marketability of our Percaarisus Permentol line. Let me clear up some misunderstandings: Our continued, concentrated research over the past 18 months shows this line, without a doubt, to be effective in treating the symptoms for which it was developed.

But I will acknowledge difficulty you may have in selling such an innovative approach to treatment. To this end, let me remind you that we have test kits for you to offer the customer so that he can gather and examine results for himself. Please order and deliver these test kits;

without them, you will have trouble in selling this product until more publicity has been done.

Concentrated effort will mean additional time zeroing in on primary markets; but once you qualify your leads, you will begin to pick up additional customers and enjoy substantial commissions. If you need help in qualifying specific leads, contact Frank Bohon.

Because a negative attitude always diminishes your selling success, I hope this will clear up any concerns you may have had about test results. I look forward to seeing sales of this new line on your next reports.

Do's

- State the rumor and the "correction" upfront.
- Acknowledge tidbits of truth from which almost all rumors have their origin. Such acknowledgment adds credibility to your explanations, corrections, or denials. In this memo, note that the writer acknowledges difficulty selling an innovative, unpublicized breakthrough that some may still consider "unproven."
- If the rumor is damaging, emphasize the importance of "keeping the record straight."
- Be tactful about wording; no one likes to be considered a gossiper or rumormonger. Notice the substitution of the word "concerns" for "rumors" in the above example.
- End with a positive, business-as-usual closing.

SAFETY PRECAUTIONS

Good Models

Subject: Tumbler Safety Violation

On October 6, in passing through the BD area, I found rubber bands again wrapped around the limit-switch button on #233 tumbler to keep the switch activated while the dust cover was removed.

Please stop this practice immediately. Having the dust cover and guard in place prevents operators from getting a head or limb hung or struck by this heavy rotating equipment.

In addition to your own safety, keep in mind that this is also a violation of company policy.

Please sign and return this memo to me.

◆ ◆ ◆

Subject: Safety Precaution--Proper Storage

I'd like to emphasize the fact that plant aisles should not be used for storage of any kind. Equipment, goods, and supplies stored in the aisles not only block passage but also increase the likelihood of accidents.

A case in point: While waiting to punch the time clock, an employee standing on a skid with a loose board slipped and struck his back on the skid. Apparently the skid, loaded with boxes of samples from the lab, had been placed in the aisle for temporary storage.

To prevent reoccurrence of a similar accident and to make your operation smoother, please observe the following safety precautions:
* Do not store anything in the aisles.
* Call Maintenance to arrange transport of bulky items that you cannot move yourself.
* Ask me to assign extra storage space when a large shipment of supplies or equipment cannot be contained in your area.

Thank you for cooperating with us in maintaining a safe workplace.

Do's _____

- Highlight the unsafe practice immediately.
- Include the reason, unless the reason is flagrantly obvious, for your precaution. Remember that the standard attitude about safety precautions

seems to be, "Accidents happen to other people, not me." Citing past incidents or injury statistics adds authority and credibility to your concern.

● When readers do not accept reasons behind the precautions as legitimate, remind them of safety precautions as company policy.

● Suggest safe alternatives to correct any problem or situation that has or may lead to safety violations.

● Sound positive and confident of cooperation.

SEASONAL GREETINGS

Good Models

Subject: Best Wishes for the Holiday Season

As we approach the holiday season, I want to take this opportunity to express my appreciation for your loyal, productive efforts over the past 12 months.

Working with a group of professionals such as you, who care about the job you do and the people you work with, is a pleasure I don't take for granted.

My best wishes to you and your families for a safe, happy holiday season.

◆　◆　◆

Subject: Best Wishes for the New Year

During this past year, our team efforts have resulted in unprecedented growth for our company. The Utclair and Joshua contracts come readily to mind as our most significant contributions and also our most challenging. All of us, I'm sure, have gained valuable professional experience and managed to strengthen our friendships as well.

I look forward to ushering in another fulfilling year at Memorial. Have a happy holiday season.

◆　◆　◆

Subject: Holiday Cheer

Let me put my good spirit and best wishes in writing: Here's to the happiest holiday season and new year to date; you deserve it. Until the Christmas party December 23--

Do's _____

* Be brief.
* Focus on the employees as individuals. You may do this by calling them by name, mentioning specific team accomplishments or "problems"

handled in the past year, commenting on any holiday plans to get together, or looking forward to any new projects in the coming year.

● Be sincere. A "routine" greeting sounds as though it came from a machine. To be sincere, be specific and creative.

SOLICITATIONS
(of financial/personal involvement)

Weak Model

Subject: Blood Drive

As you all know, it's that time of the year again--blood drive, January 23 and 24. All of you have already received a pamphlet explaining the procedure; please fill out the attached form and return it to me by Wednesday, January 18.

I have to account for every individual in the department, so please return the form regardless of whether you do or do not plan to donate.

Don'ts

- Don't make this a "routine," business-as-usual memo. You need to get attention either by your style of writing or by other motivational tactics.
- Don't sound as though your own involvement is obligatory.
- Don't take for granted that your reader will understand the benefits of participation.

Good Models

Subject: Flower Fund

If you're reading this, you're not laid up in the hospital and next in line to receive a nice fragrant bouquet of flowers meant to say you're missed while away.

But just in case--the flower fund needs to be replenished. All contributions are voluntary, of course; but if you wish to donate, contact Sandy Sherron, who holds the money bag. Two dollars per person should hold us in the black for a while longer.

As a reminder, let me mention again that departmental policy is to send flowers to an employee or his/her spouse when confinement exceeds four days. Also, a memorial gift or flowers are sent to the family in the event of the death of an employee or a member of his immediate family.

Come on, gang, and let's chip in to be that "extended family" that means so much in time of sickness or death.

◆ ◆ ◆

Subject: AVA Symposium Participation

The fall 198- symposium of the AVA has been scheduled for September 23 and 24 in Kansas City. With great anticipation, I'd like to ask you to be a part of that symposium by presenting a 45-minute talk on product packaging. If you agree to participate, I'll be forwarding a complete program of topics and times in a few weeks.

With your expertise developed over the past 10 years, we feel you're well qualified to speak on the subject, and we more than ever need to hear what you have to offer us in the way of packaging guidelines. Additionally, I might add that this forum is an excellent one to promote your division's views on all our products and packaging. We expect approximately 50 representatives companywide.

Other speakers include T. A. Smith, Y. E. Yates, J. H. Hilton, and M. K. Chu. Topics have not yet been narrowed down clearly; however, all will revolve around the theme of targeting the proper market. Of course, AVA will cover your expenses; they will not be billed back to your own department.

I look forward to your answer as soon as possible.

◆ ◆ ◆

Subject: New Departmental Publication

Have you ever wondered what supervisors Jack Bright and Sarah Gomez do in their spare time? You might be surprised to find out while reading a new monthly departmental newsletter, Tales-N-Techniques, to make its first appearance in June.

Tales-N-Techiques is designed to keep employees informed about departmental issues as well as each other. In the "techniques" section of the newsletter, we hope to discuss current technical problems and offer suggestions for their solution. In the "tales" section, we'd like to feature various employees who are involved in volunteer civic activities.

Here's how you can help: When you stumble onto a problem and work out a solution with the new equipment or discover a new application that has significance for the department as a whole, let us know. Also, keep your ears open for tales of employees in this or other locations who are involved in volunteer programs like Big Brothers/Big Sisters or Meals on Wheels. Please forward these feature tips on techniques or people to our new editor, Larry Sanders, at extension 4670.

This is your newsletter; we want it to serve your interests. Help us help you stay informed, solve problems, and get to know the person at the next desk.

And stay tuned for the latest developments on Jack and Sarah. . . .

Do's

- Use a teaser, or at least upbeat, first statement or paragraph to get attention and compete with more pressing tasks. Then state your request for participation.
- Be explicit in what kind of response you expect; give the details the reader needs to respond. Make things easy.
- Elaborate on incentives for involvement. Mention specific personal benefits when you can; suggest departmental or company goodwill when you must be general.
- Give testimonials, if possible, from higher-ups who intend to particpate and who support your efforts. If not sheer enthusiasm, then obligation and politics may provide the necessary incentive. Notice that in the AVA Symposium memo, the names of other higher-ranking speakers have been listed to add "clout" to the request.
- Show personal enthusiasm for the project.
- Write in a light, informal style on most occasions. Personal involvement most often results when people who care about people convey personal warmth and concern.

SPECIFICATIONS

Good Models

Subject: Description of the Spectrograph (Monochromator) Body

The spectrograph is an optical instrument used to perform qualitative or semiquantitative chemical analyses based on intensities of spectral lines emitted by excited atoms.

The <u>body</u> of the spectrograph consists of a large brass cylinder, 48 inches long, $16\frac{1}{2}$ inches outside diameter, and $\frac{1}{4}$ inch wall thickness. This cylinder is closed at each end and has provision for attaching a diffusion pump and a vacuum gauge (an ionization gauge).

The two END PLATES on the cylinder and the two 1 5/8-inch-wide FLANGES, 19 inches in diameter, are made of 1-inch-thick Muntz metal. Muntz metal is an alloy consisting of 60 percent copper and 40 percent zinc.

Each FLANGE contains a $\frac{1}{4}$-inch-deep groove so that it can be fitted snugly over the ends of the cylindrical body. On the opposite side of each flange is a groove, 0.206 ± 0.003 inch wide. A Parker O-ring seal, size 2-461, 16-inch inside diameter, $\frac{1}{4}$-inch thickness, made of butyl rubber base (material number E 515-8), can be placed into the groove for proper vacuum sealing with the end plate.

Each flange and end plate has 12 equally spaced $\frac{1}{4}$-inch holes drilled through it. These holes are centered on an 18 1/8-inch-diameter bolt circle. Each flange is secured to the cylindrical body with tin-lead solder.

The end plates are held in alignment with the flanges by means of two large steel HINGES. These hinges enable one person to open the spectrograph and swing the end plates out of the work area without strain. Each hinge is fastened to the back side of an end flange with four $\frac{1}{4}$-inch-diameter, $1\frac{1}{4}$-inch-long bolts.

When an O-ring has been seated in the groove of a flange, the end plate swings into position so that its machined surface is flat against the O-ring. The 12 bolts can then be tightened to a torque of $8\frac{1}{2}$ foot-pounds so the O-ring is compressed into the groove by the end plate, thus making a vacuum-tight seal.

Two pieces of $\frac{1}{2}$-inch-thick aluminum, alloy 2024-T351, are used to provide a SHELF. The aluminum pieces are held together, side by side, by three cleats on the underside. The shelf is 15 inches wide and therefore rests below the center of the cylindrical cross section of the body. The shelf's length is 42½ inches. This length allows 1 inch of space between the end of the shelf and the front-end plate and 4 inches' space at the rear end. Thus, pumping speed is not retarded by the presence of the shelf.

◆ ◆ ◆

Subject: Specifications for Pile Hammer

1. Pile hammers used to install cylinder piles shall be capable of developing a rated energy per blow of no less than 122,000 joules (90,000 foot-pounds). The hammer shall have a minimum ram weight of 27,215 kilograms (65,000 pounds) and an adjustable stroke.
2. The hammer shall be equipped with a capblock composed of alternating layers of aluminum and Micarta plates. The layers will cushion the blow of the ram on the follower.
3. Followers shall cover the entire head of the cylinder pile, maintaining concentricity between the hammer and pile, efficiently transmitting blow energy from hammer to pile, and enclosing an acceptable wood cushion to protect the head of the pile during driving.
4. A wood cushion block at least 152mm (6 inches) thick shall be used on the head of the pile to distribute the hammer-to-blow energy uniformly. The cushion block shall be composed of layers of 19mm-thick plywood or an acceptable alternate as approved by the designer. The dimension shall be such as to cover completely the concrete cross section of the pile.

Don'ts

• Don't include a "Scope of Work" section. Its usual vagueness makes it meaningless and dangerous. Like other introductions, "Scope of Work" sections tend to be padding that says simply, "Later I'm going to tell you something important and specific." Yet these sections can be dangerous: Readers may glance at the section thinking they have the whole picture and later find "minor" surprises surfacing in the detailed sections. When "Scope of Work" sections are at their best—specific—they become redundant.

• Don't use all-encompassing catchclauses such as the following: "The company shall complete and include everything for full operation of the system with all work subject to approval by our engineers." Open to many interpretations, such comments usually mean, "Guess what may turn up later that I want you to do."

• Don't add "etc." at the end of a list. This suggests that the writer doesn't know what the list consists of or is too lazy to finish the writing. The "etc." only raises questions.

Do's

(NOTE: Because specifications vary so widely from subject to subject, all of the following "do's" won't apply in every case.)

● Take care with assumptions about your readers' knowledge. Almost always with specifications, you will be writing for more than one reader. Know their background, knowledge, and recent familiarity with your subject. When in doubt, explain.

● Overview the objectives of a process, project, or equipment before beginning specific details. Notice the first paragraph in the spectograph memo.

● Try to pinpoint and briefly state the number of stages, steps, or components in the process, instruction, or description. Such breakdowns make the entire subject more understandable. Note the capped words that serve as headings to break the spectograph assembly into phases.

● In describing equipment, begin with the internal parts and move to the outer or vice versa, whichever arrangement seems more logical. However, don't move back and forth between the two detail arrangements.

● Define unfamiliar terms the first time you use them. How do you know in this technical field which terms are unfamiliar? Again, knowing your audience is essential. In general, it's always better to give an "unnecessary" definition than to omit a necessary one. In the first memo, the writer defines which type of "vacuum gauge" and also the content of "Muntz metal."

● Use abbreviations to cut word length, but make sure they are standard and well known.

● Mention prominently any safety precautions and repeat again before the step or section in which the precaution should be taken.

● Give steps in chronological order. Indicate each step in a separate sentence. Otherwise, the steps may be understood as simultaneous rather than separate, sequential actions.

● Write instructions in the imperative mood: "Monitor these compasses for . . ." rather than, "These compasses should be monitored for . . ." "Cover the abutting end surfaces with an approved sealing material" rather than, "The abutting end surfaces shall be covered with an approved sealing material."

● Make text and drawings complement rather than duplicate each other. For instance, in the text you may tell how a tube clamps onto a reduction fitting and give the tube dimensions in the drawing. The problem in repeating information in two places is twofold: 1) Either the drawing or the text may be changed at some later date without accompanying changes in the other document, thus resulting in contradictory details. 2) The same information may be reworded for "clarification," thus resulting in two separate interpretations. If you need to repeat information in two places, make sure your wording is an exact repetition.

● Place supporting table, sketches, charts, photographs, or lists as close to their mention in the text as possible.

● Use numerals instead of written numbers.

● Give kinds, classes, or grades of materials in a manner that permits you to be specific for all situations. To do this, begin with the exceptions and then lump into "all the rest" categories. For example:

Pipe: 3/8 inch for lavoratories and water fountains; ½ inch for all sprinkler systems; 3/4 inch *for all other* water lines.

● Break up long blocks of text. Use frequent section or paragraph titles; use lists; or put key words or phrases in capital letters, italicize them, or underline them. These aids allow your reader to skim as with a reference manual or legal document without reading large blocks of text. Highlight significant details by placing them alone in a separate, short paragraph.

SYMPATHY

Good Model

(NOTE: Sympathy notes should be written in longhand on personal stationery—even when the condolences are from everyone in a department.)

Subject: Memorial Donation in the Name of Eva Wilson

Jack, our department was so sorry to hear of the automobile accident and Eva's death. I remember meeting her at the organizational Christmas banquet last year, and at that time thinking what a warm, intelligent person she was. In fact, we talked of your plans to move into the position you now hold. From what you've said of her, too, I know she must have provided inspiration, meaning, and emotional support in so many of your career accomplishments. I can only imagine what a great loss this will be to you and your two boys.

All of us here in the office want to express our sympathy by making a contribution to the American Heart Fund in your name. If you can think of anything that we can do as far as notifying other colleagues or clients please let us know.

Do's

- Mention the tragedy about which you are writing, but avoid going into detail of the situation, its consequences, or how you heard of the incident.
- Let the reader know that you understand his loss by mentioning specific details and praise of the deceased. When you don't know the deceased well, speak of "hearsay" evidence or remind the reader of complimentary things he himself has said of the loved one: "I've heard you say that . . ." Such comments help the reader to praise the loved one and to work through his own grief.
- If you offer help, be specific. General offers ("if there's anything I can do to help") sound insincere.
- Express your sympathy with action (donations, flowers, referrals, whatever) if you can do so.

THANK YOUS
(for advice, hospitality, information, a raise, completion of a project)

Good Models

Subject: Thank You for June 14 Conference

Ms. Henley, thank you for giving me so much of your time last Monday afternoon and for your welcome advice on my career advancement.

I did follow up on both of your suggestions. Bob Holloway has asked me to come to work on his new project; I'll be assuming those new responsibilities after the first of the month. Also, I notified Training of my interest in the upcoming computer course, and due to a last-minute cancellation, I am enrolled to attend next week.

Please know how much I appreciate your interest in my studies and career advancement.

◆   ◆   ◆

Subject: Florida Hospitality

Harvey, just a note to say thank you for your hospitality while I was soaking up the sunny southern atmosphere and doing my homework in learning to fine-tune a MOG system. Do tell your wife thanks for giving up her evening alone with you and joining us for Tuesday night's "fiesta."

Please let me repay the favor when you're out our way next fall; I know of a skeet-shooting range you would enjoy. If you let me know a day or two in advance, I'll make the arrangements.

Thanks again.

◆   ◆   ◆

Subject: Leads on TeleChange

You and Sylvia Koonzt are to be commended on the excellent cooperation you've given the home office in furnishing qualified leads on the TeleChange. We have passed these leads on to the appropriate people (Harriet Stovall and Mark Browning), and they have been able to make all three sales.

Sylvia, I'm sure, will be expressing her thanks to you directly. As a result of these sales, she has surpassed her yearly sales objectives with two months still to go.

We know that passing on these leads took extra time from your daily effort, and we want you to know that we appreciate and have noted the support. Keep up the good work.

◆　◆　◆

Subject:　Company Picnic

I want to express my appreciation for your help in making the company picnic such a success. In the factory setting, we all sometimes lose sight of each other as people who can enrich our lives on a personal level. I very much enjoy the opportunity to meet staff families and to relax in an away-from-work atmosphere. Certainly, your colleagues, from the many comments I overheard last Saturday, appreciate your efforts for the same reasons.

I know this took a great deal of time from the beginning stages back in March, through the April publicity campaign, and finally with the nitty-gritty details of catering arrangements and whatnot. Would you especially thank Joe Navarone for lending his volleyball equipment and Jim Pederson for handling the cleanup detail.

A fine job from all of you. If I can be of some service to you in the future, please call on me.

◆　◆　◆

Subject:　Merit Raise

I'd like to thank you for the merit raise effective June 1. I take this as an indication that you and upper management appreciate my efforts and are concerned about my future here. To the best of my abilities, I intend to be worthy of that confidence and will do everything in my power to meet the objectives outlined in my 198- Activity Plan submitted last week.

Please know that I am eager to take on any additional responsibilities that develop in this area and will incorporate them into "the scheme of things" around this office. Thanks for your personal support and encouragement.

Do's

- State your "thank you" immediately as the primary reason for writing.
- Be specific in detailing the "whys" of your thankfulness. In other words, let the reader know that you understand and appreciate the efforts he put forth.

- Mention the good results of the reader's information, advice, or project. What benefits did you or someone else derive? Omit any disastrous results that would detract from the thanks.
- Name names; thank individuals, not groups.
- In the case of a raise, write as though you have received a reward for work well done; show both confidence and humility.

TRAINING
(announcements, selections, confirmations)

Good Models

Subject: Fire-Safety Training

You are asked to attend one session of a fire-safety training program to be held in the second-floor conference room, July 15, 16, and 17.

Because seating in the conference room is limited, please call Mary Paxton at extension 2668 if you must arrange to attend a session other than the one designated below:

Traffic Control	9:00 to 11:00 a.m., July 15
Security	9:00 to 11:00 a.m., July 16
Maintenance	9:00 to 11:00 a.m., July 17

The emphasis of this year's meeting is safety in high-rise buildings, with a discussion of special safety features in the Merimac Tower. Mike Spartan will conduct this mandatory training for all employees.

◆ ◆ ◆

Subject: Course Offering--"Effective Presentations"

The Training Department is offering a new two-day seminar, "Effective Presentations," scheduled May 5-6, 198-, 8:00 a.m. to 5:00 p.m. both days. If you would like members of your staff to attend, please submit their names in writing or by phone (ext. 4471) by April 15.

This course is open to all employees and particularly helpful to those who make upper-management presentations.

Participants in the workshop will—
* develop additional knowledge in planning, researching, organizing, and presenting information to a group;
* learn the mechanics and helpful hints in using easels, flip charts, viewgraphs, 35mm slides, and handouts;
* gain insight into techniques of persuasion;
* identify ways to use group feedback.

Each attendee will receive a notebook of materials as later reference for planning, preparing, and delivering presentations.

"Effective Presentations" will be conducted by Ida Flowers, a consultant with Emitz Consulting Group. She has had 10 years' experience in the field and comes highly recommended by other clients such as Grayco Corporation, International DataCorp, and Porterfield-Waggoner.

Her course outline, with her methods explained, is attached. Please note that participants will be given adequate class time to practice the skills taught.

We have confidence that this consultant-led seminar will deliver the results it promises.

◆   ◆   ◆

Subject: Scheduling and Confirmation of Communication Skills
            Workshop

You have been selected to attend the Communication Skills Workshop, February 7-11, at Houston headquarters offices, conference room C-123. Please call to confirm your reservation by February 1. If I do not hear from you, I will assume you have had a change of plans since your supervisor nominated you and will assign another employee to the workshop in your place.

So that the program can be tailored to meet your individual needs, please bring with you at least three writing samples. You will critique and rework these in class. Additionally, you will need to read the enclosed booklet and prepare a case study from your on-the-job experience; complete instructions for the case study are given in the booklet. Please do not attend the class unless you have completed this pre-workshop assignment.

This workshop focuses on both oral and written communication skills, both of which you will have opportunity to practice during the week. Objectives include the following:
* Identify barriers to effective communication and examine causes
* Assess personal attitudes toward supervisory communication skills
* Explore feedback--what it is, what it is not, how to give and receive it
* Improve clarity of written materials
* Condense length of written materials
* Develop organizational techniques for both verbal and written communications

The workshop will meet Monday through Friday from 8:00 a.m. to 5:00 p.m. You must attend all five sessions to receive training credit.

Feel free to call our staff instructor, Margaret Anderson (ext. 3999), with questions regarding your preparation, her workshop objectives and methods, or scheduling arrangements. Ms. Anderson has been presenting this course for the past six years; evaluations from participants continue to rate the course "excellent."

Do's

- Be sure to direct the correct message to the correct audience. If the memo is a confirmation, highlight the instructions and details upfront.
- Distinguish between the needs and interests of your two primary audiences—participants, and supervisors of participants. Supervisors will be most interested in the course objectives and results promised. Participants will have additional interests, such as preparation required, methods of instruction, and details of confirming and attending.
- Give *all* details of the training program (dates, hours, locations) in all correspondence rather than "parceling them out" when you think readers need to know—a few in the course brochure, a few in the course scheduling announcement, and finally a few in the confirmation memo. On occasion, participants' attendance depends on their ability to schedule flights and end other meetings and projects within a limited time frame. From the start, give them all the details that may affect their registration.
- Highlight course objectives in announcements. Never take for granted that supervisors have a knowledge of the course—even if it has been offered before. And never assume that supervisors pass on these course objectives to participants they nominate for training.
- Establish the credibility of the instructor. Course effectiveness in most cases depends on the authority and skill of the instructor. Both participants and their supervisors deserve to know who will be leading the learning effort.
- Mention the intended audience—if not already obvious from the memo's distribution list or course description. Is the course most helpful to midmanagement people, entry-level employees, those with 10 years' experience of more, those who handle certain kinds of tasks?
- Be firm about expected preparation.

TRANSMITTALS

Good Models

Subject: Audit of Eastern Division, Australia

We have completed our review of Eastern Division, Australia, for the year ended Decemer 31, 198-; our full report is attached.

Our audit revealed weaknesses in the following areas:
* Case disbursements--The Blodgett plant does not cancel vendor invoices to prevent possible duplicate payments.
* Inventories--There are no written instructions on how supplies are counted, documented, summarized, or used.
* Payroll--Numerous employees' wages have been charged to the incorrect vessel.

We feel that our detailed recommendations in the enclosed report require serious attention in the immediate future. Please reply to us by March 15 about the action taken toward these recommendations.

We sincerely appreciate the assistance given our auditor, Jill Johnson, while she was in your area.

◆ ◆ ◆

Subject: Company Telephone Use

Attached for your information only is a copy of a computer run listing each employee under your supervision, his or her extension number, and telephone calls for the previous month. This information will inform you of amounts being charged to your department monthly and allow you to curb any unnecessary calls.

◆ ◆ ◆

Subject: Court Order #891-DG-11
             Grand Rapids, Michigan

The attached copy of the court order #891-DG-11 regarding our property at Grand Rapids, Michigan, comes at the request of D. J. Hougser.

You'll notice that some items show "no address"; we have attempted to mail these payments to the last known address, but to no avail. Should you be able to locate any of these addresses, let us know so that we can mail checks immediately.

◆   ◆   ◆

Subject: Additions/Revisions to <u>Financial and Accounting Methods Manual</u>

Enclosed are additions/revisions to United's <u>Financial and Accounting Methods Manual</u>. An attached list of topics provides section numbers and pages that have been added or revised. For revisions, please remove the previous subject material and note the changes made to the policy/procedure. For additions, place the new topics in the appropriate manual section.

As a reminder, each manual holder is responsible for maintaining updated appendixes on all topics, whether mailed with this quarterly distribution or under separate cover. If you have any questions in adding these pages to your manual, please contact me.

◆   ◆   ◆

Subject: Schedule of Common Stock Dividend Information

At your request, I have attached a complete history of the common stock dividends of Fairway, Inc., from its inception to the present.

The information presented reflects all three stock splits (in 1958, 1969, and 1983).

◆   ◆   ◆

Subject: Memorial LEG Agreements

We are providing the attached documents concerning Memorial, as you requested by phone on April 26, 198-.
    1. Shareholders Agreement dated February 10, 198-
    2. Amendment to LEG contract dated March 10, 198-
    3. Endorsement #3 to Shareholders Agreement dated March 10, 198-
    4. Letter from D. J. Stanley dated April 4, 198-

Should you have any questions about these, please refer them to Martha Harvey in the Legal Department, extension 1184.

◆   ◆   ◆

Subject: RRE Properties

Attached for your processing is check #1566 for $2,200; we received this from RRE Properties as advance payment for preliminary engineering work, order #4499.

The estimated cost of total work on this order is $8,666; upon receipt of RRE Properties' check for the remaining amount, we will forward it to your office for processing.

◆   ◆   ◆

Subject: AFE #MT9-991--Installation of Equipment to Serve Tidwell, Inc.

Enclosed are five copies of the preliminary invoice #MT9-991 for $776,000. This represents our engineer's estimated AFE cost.

The AFE actual cost to date exceeds the engineering estimate; however, late charges, rental charges, and surplus-material refunds will need to be taken into account before we forward the final invoice.

If this invoice amount meets with your approval, please forward it to Harrington Corporation and send us a copy of your transmittal letter for our records.

Do's _____

- Mention the information you are transmitting first; this document, illustration, printout, check, invoice, or report *is* the major message of interest. (Ordinarily, in other memo categories, you mention attachments last.)
- List all enclosures specifically to discover errors with regard to missing documents or improperly routed documents.
- Tell why the document is being sent. Is it at the reader's request? For information only? To verify your own records? For processing? For approval? For distribution?
- Give a brief summary of the significant information contained in the attached document. Depending on the document, this summary may mean only the amount of a check or invoice and its purpose, or a lengthy paragraph about major findings contained in a complex report.
- Anticipate and answer possible questions about the attachments: Are there unusual figures or facts that the reader may question? Are there omissions? If so, why? Will there be exceptions? If so, what are they?
- Give your opinion, when appropriate, about the enclosed information. Do the enclosed meeting minutes show progress in the negotiations? Do you

think the entire project will be completed by the target date? Do you agree with the disputed invoice you're submitting? In other words, prepare and/or interpret for the reader.

● If you're not sending all the reader needs or has asked for, tell him why not. Then let him know when to expect further information or documents.

WELCOMES

Good Model

Subject: Welcome to Pantego-Morris

With enthusiasm, we welcome you to Pantego-Morris. Recruiting only the most capable people such as you is one of the most enjoyable and rewarding of my responsibilities.

We all look forward to your contributions of creative publicity--particularly on the Jamison account--and innovative marketing strategies. To paraphrase a cliche, five heads are better than four. After your first Thursday-morning staff meeting, you'll see that we really do work together as a team.

Of course, your first few days on the job will be taxing, but remember that help is only a desk away. When you have questions about the job or the thousand-and-one other things in relocating a wife, three children, and a collie, just ask.

You've made a sound choice in coming to Pantego-Morris, and we'll do everything possible to provide you with opportunities for career growth. Here's to a long and rewarding relationship.

Do's

- Show sincere enthusiasm and confidence in the prospective employee.
- Make the reader feel good about the decision to join the staff, with gentle reminders about the challenges and rewards of the future.
- Be gracious in offering specific help to orient the employee to the team and the physical environment.
- Use an informal tone.
- Personalize your message. You may mention the employee's background or credentials or future assignments, his efforts in relocating, or success in adjustment for other family members. Whatever personal comments you make will lift the memo from the abstract welcome mat sent to "Everyman."